THE VULNERABILITY WORKBOOK

Embrace Fear, Set Boundaries, and Find the Courage to Live Greatly

ANOUARE ABDOU

Published by:
Ulysses Press
PO Box 3440
Berkeley, CA 94703
www.ulyssespress.com

ISBN: 978-1-64604-403-0
Library of Congress Control Number: 2022936266

Printed in the United States by Versa Press
10 9 8 7 6 5 4 3 2 1

Acquisitions editor: Kierra Sondereker
Managing editor: Claire Chun
Editor: Phyllis Elving
Proofreader: Renee Rutledge
Front cover design: Rebecca Lown
Interior design: what!design @ whatweb.com
Layout: Winnie Liu

IMPORTANT NOTE TO READERS: This book has been written and published for informational and educational purposes only. It is not intended to serve as medical advice or to be any form of medical treatment. You should always consult with your physician before altering or changing any aspect of your medical treatment. Do not stop or change any prescription medications without the guidance and advice of your physician. Any use of the information in this book is made on the reader's good judgment and is the reader's sole responsibility. This book is not intended to diagnose or treat any medical condition and is not a substitute for a physician. This book is independently authored and published and no sponsorship or endorsement of this book by, and no affiliation with, any trademarked brands or other products mentioned within is claimed or suggested. All trademarks that appear in this book belong to their respective owners and are used here for informational purposes only. The author and publisher encourage readers to patronize the brands mentioned in this book.

To my partner Dan, who inspires me to keep showing up with vulnerability.

CONTENTS

CHAPTER 4: PRACTICING AUTHENTIC COMMUNICATION . . 69

CHAPTER 5: ESTABLISHING HEALTHY BOUNDARIES 88

CHAPTER 6: ANCHORING SELF-TRUST 106

CHAPTER 7: MANAGING INTENSE EMOTIONS 125

CHAPTER 8: USING YOUR DISCERNMENT 140

CHAPTER 9: HOLDING SPACE FOR OTHERS 160

CHAPTER 10: REFLECTING ON WHAT YOU'VE LEARNED AND RECOMMITTING. 175

ACKNOWLEDGMENTS 190

ABOUT THE AUTHOR 191

INTRODUCTION

Vulnerability equals death. Sounds pretty dramatic, right? But being vulnerable is the state of being exposed to a threat, and as human beings with a powerful survival instinct, we naturally seek to limit our exposure to threats. Predictability, on the other hand, ensures safety—because what we can predict, we can try to control. So predictability means survival, while threats are unpredictable. Predictability brings comfort, while threats breed fear.

What you do when exposed to this universal fear of vulnerability, and how you seek comfort to bring yourself back to the safety of predictability, determines your quality of life. The opportunities you pursue. The range of emotions you allow yourself to feel. The depth of your connection with yourself, others, and the world. It's the difference between a life worth living and one filled with regrets. Emancipation or a self-imposed prison.

Embracing vulnerability is the bridge that can take you to the life and relationships of your dreams. The greater your capacity to understand vulnerability and lean into it in appropriate and constructive ways, the greater your capacity to experience profound joy, love, authenticity, and fulfillment. Here's the catch, though: it's going to feel uncomfortable and, at times, unnatural.

How the Fear of Vulnerability Shows Up in Your Life

Imagine this: Your boss announces that she is leaving. Her position is going to be open, and your coworkers are already gossiping about who is going to apply for the job. You feel a little spark of desire. You have experience, and you've harbored ideas about what it would be like to be in your boss's shoes. But now that the opportunity is real and you have the possibility of applying for the job, your heart races and your gut flutters at the very thought of putting your name up for a promotion.

You've just felt the vulnerability of potential failure. It would be terrifying to apply for the job and not get it. It would also be scary to get the job and mess it up—what if you weren't truly capable of pulling it off? So you don't apply.

Now think about having a crush. The delicious daydreams. Putting together an outfit that makes you feel amazing and hoping you'll run into this person. Your pulse accelerates during a moment of eye contact. You would love to go on a date, but you haven't been asked out. Yet the thought of expressing your interest makes you want to vomit. What if you are seen as just a friend? So you don't say anything. And that is the vulnerability of potential rejection.

These scenarios are examples of fearing vulnerability. You are terrified of the pain associated with possible outcomes, such as failure or rejection. So you adjust your behavior to reduce your emotional exposure to those threats and mitigate the risk of pain. That takes the form of avoiding certain actions, such as applying for the job or asking your crush out.

But vulnerability can also look like a direct action, such as breaking up with someone before they break up with you. Or holding yourself to impossible standards, trying to be more attractive, more successful, and smarter in the quest of acceptance.

Vulnerability feels like a loss of control, and your reaction may be an attempt to take back control, steering yourself away from threat and toward safety. However, your attempts to keep yourself safe can end up harming you. Maybe you would have gotten that promotion. Maybe you could have married the crush you never ended up dating. Maybe you end up successful, smart, beautiful—but miserable and alone.

The Benefits of Embracing Vulnerability

If embracing vulnerability is good for you but emotional exposure feels nearly unbearable, are you bound to experience intense levels of discomfort every time you try to be vulnerable?

Yes and no. In this workbook, you'll learn how to feel safer while being vulnerable. And that includes knowing when it's appropriate to be vulnerable, and at what level. At the end of the day, those feelings of discomfort associated with emotional exposure are necessary for survival. You wouldn't stay in a burning building—you'd run for the exit. So you need discernment and self-trust in order to green-light vulnerability. It's not an all-or-nothing thing. With some parameters in place, it will feel safer to hold space for your state of vulnerability (and the vulnerability of others)—and you may even reach a point where it feels amazing.

In this workbook you'll acquire tools to get out of your comfort zone despite all the *ickiness* you experience when being vulnerable. That might include taking an action that feels scary or doing something that doesn't feel intuitive at first. You will learn to accept that the feeling of sheer terror that can come with vulnerability never completely goes away. Discomfort is part of it, but you'll become more comfortable with the uncomfortable.

The benefits of tackling such courageous inner work—and you are courageous for even opening this book—include increased self-acceptance, greater authenticity, a fuller experience of life, and relationships that are richer and more meaningful.

The beauty of this process is that you can't work on vulnerability without accepting the parts of yourself that you've deemed too flawed to examine, let alone show to others. You can't lean into vulnerability without honoring what is true and authentic for *you*. You can't explore vulnerability without going to places you've never been before, some more exhilarating than you could ever have imagined. And finally, it would be impossible to cultivate vulnerability without noticing an immediate positive impact on the love you are able to give and receive. All of this makes the work worthwhile.

Included in this workbook are action tools to help you deconstruct vulnerability and turn it into a practice that will enrich your life and your relationships. From setting a vision for your vulnerability journey and cultivating self-awareness to building shame resilience and practicing authentic communication, you will explore 10 core pillars of vulnerability. First, through examples of interpersonal situations, you will learn why each of these pillars is important and how it shows up in real life. Then you will practice putting that pillar into action in your own life through self-reflection exercises (such as journaling prompts) as well as specific concrete actions.

Ready to dive deep? Just bring an open mind and a brave heart. A willingness to see and do things differently. And prepare for discomfort, knowing that there will be great rewards on the other side. Besides that, all you'll need is a pen.

Chapter 1

SETTING A VISION AND INTENTIONS FOR YOUR VULNERABILITY JOURNEY

American professor of literature Joseph Campbell is most famous for his work on the hero's journey, breaking down the stages of story and inner transformation that a hero undergoes while on a quest.[1] If choosing to live with vulnerability instead of running away from it is an act of courage, you can think of yourself as a hero. And if you are reading this book, you've already experienced the first step of your hero's journey: the call to adventure.

This is the moment when you are faced with a challenge or a conflict that disrupts the equilibrium of your day-to-day life and forces you into action. Your adventure begins. You leave behind what is familiar and comfortable and embark on an expedition filled with adversity but also opportunity and helpful resources, such as mentors and guides. You will ultimately conquer your obstacles and emerge victorious—and be profoundly changed in the process.

Regardless of whatever external event might have moved you to pick up this book, you probably didn't stumble upon the idea of working on vulnerability by accident. For most people, the decision to prioritize vulnerability is a call to adventure forced by some external event, such as a painful breakup or an inability to experience nourishing relationships. It's not the kind of stuff they teach you in school, yet it's an essential life skill. And there comes a moment when you realize you can no longer go through the motions of life without it. And so your journey begins.

Before slaying any metaphorical dragons, though, it's important to set a vision and arm yourself with intentions. Heroes in mythical journeys are able to persevere through difficulties because they have a strong "why." They need to save their community. Reunite with a soulmate. Acquire some object.

---

1 Joseph Campbell, *The Hero with a Thousand Faces* (Novato, California: New World Library, 2008).

THE **VULNERABILITY** WORKBOOK

Whatever the case may be, it's the ultimate outcome of the adventure that matters—an outcome a hero will go to great lengths to achieve.

When learning how to understand, embrace, and put into action the idea of being vulnerable, you'll experience ups and downs. Without a clear vision in mind, you might be tempted to give up and revert to your old ways. That's why it's essential to remember your ultimate desire and keep going.

In this chapter you will be setting a vision and intentions for your personal vulnerability journey. By the end of the chapter, once you've completed the exercises it includes, you'll understand your own desired outcome. You'll feel connected to that outcome and motivated by it. You'll truly understand what your call to adventure is all about.

You'll also be armed with a set of guiding principles that can act as your compass on this adventure. Keep in mind that when you're practicing vulnerability in the real world, you'll interact with people who won't always be as well equipped as you are to engage vulnerably, so you'll need to lead the way. Fear not, though—this workbook is your ally and a resource that you can get back to at any point.

Getting Clear about Your Vulnerability Vision

Ready to start setting a vision for the ultimate outcome on your journey? Start by going through the case studies that follow. Answer the prompts to analyze the situation in each case study and identify common vulnerability pitfalls and their consequences. You can use those insights to determine what you want to experience in your life and relationships through the power of vulnerability.

CASE STUDY 1

Anna and John have been in a relationship for seven years. Since moving in together, however, the quality of their bond and their level of individual fulfillment has gone downhill. They make love less often, and when they do it feels like they are just checking a box. Date nights also feel like forced rituals, and they breathe a sigh of relief when they come back home, put on their pajamas, and get back to their respective post-work activities: watching sports on TV for John, scrolling on social media for Anna.

Anna is starting to feel increasingly resentful and dissatisfied. She longs to feel desired again and misses the spontaneity of her early dating experience with John. With an ache in her heart, she remembers the days when they couldn't get enough of each other and had profound conversations for hours. Anna often lets out her frustration by blaming John for watching too much TV and not paying enough attention to her. As a result, John tenses up whenever Anna comes home from work. He feels irritated by her presence and anticipates her next complaint. He sometimes even starts doing some chore to avoid having to talk to her.

1. In what ways does a lack of vulnerability manifest itself in Anna and John's relationship?

....

....

2. How is this lack of vulnerability contributing to their increased disconnect and dissatisfaction?

....

....

3. What could Anna do differently?

....

....

4. How could Anna lean into the fear of vulnerability to approach John?

....

....

5. What kind of different result could that lead to?

....

....

6. What could John do differently?

....

....

THE **VULNERABILITY** WORKBOOK

7. How could John lean into the fear of vulnerability to approach Anna?

....

....

8. What kind of different result could that lead to?

....

....

CASE STUDY 2

Omar is participating in a work meeting with peers and a couple of senior stakeholders from different teams, including his boss. The group is discussing unexpected issues that are preventing them from reaching their sales and customer retention targets. Poor communication between team members and department heads is leading to misunderstandings with clients. And Omar, a sales rep who deals with clients on a daily basis, has a really good idea of what could be done to improve the situation. He had even seen some of these problems coming.

Omar's boss turns to him and asks him what he thinks and whether he has any ideas to share. He feels his face flush, and all of a sudden he feels really nervous. He tells her that he doesn't have anything to add for now. She moves on to the next person, Omar's teammate Lisa, who enthusiastically shares her insights and even suggests a strategy the team could adopt. Omar's boss loves the idea and tasks Lisa with leading a project to implement her suggestion.

1. In what ways is a lack of vulnerability manifested in Omar's choice to withhold his thoughts?

....

....

2. How could this lack of vulnerability affect Omar's career?

....

....

3. How could Omar have leaned into his fear of vulnerability during this work meeting?

....

....

4. What different result could that have led to?

....

....

CASE STUDY 3

Marieke is a high-powered attorney. She works long hours, then comes back home to the glamorous apartment she'd always dreamed of as a penniless student. Her social life mainly consists of happy hours or weekend dinners with girlfriends. During those moments, she is funny and engaging. She shares sarcastic anecdotes about her coworkers and discusses her next travel plans. Sometimes her friends pour their hearts out about their stress or latest dating disasters, and Marieke encourages them or dishes out advice. But she doesn't really have much to share on that front herself—she feels just fine.

She also catches up with her family by phone from time to time, when she feels guilty about how long it has been since their last call. Her sister Irene, who is a couple of years younger than Marieke, lives in the suburbs and already has two kids. When Irene calls to talk about her struggles navigating motherhood, Marieke politely listens. But she often feels the urge to get off the phone and get back to more pressing things, like the deliverables piling up in her inbox. Her next promotion is around the corner, after all, and she often continues working well into the night while sipping a glass of wine.

1. In what ways is a lack of vulnerability manifested in Marieke's lifestyle?

....

....

2. How does it show in her relationships with friends and family?

....

....

3. How could this lack of vulnerability be affecting Marieke's life?

4. How could Marieke lean into her fear of vulnerability with her friends and family?

5. What kind of different result could that lead to?

***

Now that you've spent some time reflecting on the different ways a lack of vulnerability can manifest, you're ready to set a vision for your personal vulnerability journey. In the business world, a vision statement describes where a company aspires to be. It's about an ideal future state that gives purpose to the existence of the organization. Using the prompts below, explore the desired future state that vulnerability can help *you* achieve, and the purpose of your vulnerability journey.

1. What is the main reason you decided to get this workbook?

2. What, specifically, do you expect to get out of this workbook?

3. What's missing in your life at present?

4. What is most difficult for you when it comes to vulnerability? For example, you may find it challenging to express your feelings in relationships. Or you may struggle with the idea of losing control when showing vulnerability.

_____

_____

5. How is a fear of vulnerability holding you back?

_____

_____

6. How could embracing vulnerability benefit your life?

_____

_____

7. Complete the following sentence, thinking ahead about yourself and your life after completing this workbook. For example, "Now that I have successfully embraced vulnerability, my marriage is more fulfilling."

Now that I have successfully embraced vulnerability, _____

_____

_____.

8. What are three outcomes that would feel like absolute wins at the end of this workbook?

_____

_____

_____

THE VULNERABILITY WORKBOOK

9. Would one of those outcomes have a domino effect, automatically making the other two more achievable?

10. Where do you think you will you be 10 years from now if you achieve this outcome? How could it impact your romantic relationships?

11. How might it impact your career?

12. How will it impact your relationships with friends and family?

13. Where will you be 10 years from now if you DON'T achieve this outcome? How would this impact your romantic relationships?

14. How would it impact your career?

15. How would it impact your relationships with friends and family?

....

....

16. Why is now the best time to turn your ideal outcome into a reality?

....

....

You should now have a better idea of what you want and don't want when it comes to vulnerability and its effects on your life. It's time to craft a vision statement for your vulnerability journey! This can help you anchor yourself in your purpose while navigating the ups and downs of implementing the concepts you will learn in this workbook.

1. Close your eyes and think of the ultimate desired state that you want vulnerability to help you achieve. Sum it up in a single sentence. Need inspiration? Here are a few examples:

- "I am in the healthiest, most fulfilling relationship of my life."

- "I am closer to my family than ever before, and our relationships are getting better over time."

- "Intimacy is easy now, and I love feeling connected to myself and others."

- "I have an open heart and live boldly and with courage."

....

....

2. How will achieving this vision make you feel? Loved? Loving? Alive? Passionate? Fulfilled? Excited? List all the emotions that come up—and take a moment to feel their deliciousness.

....

....

Setting Intentions to Guide Your Vulnerability Journey

You might have heard of the concept of setting intentions. At worst, you might see it as a fluffy buzz phrase. At best, you kind of get it, but still feel that it's a bit abstract. Says author and alternative medicine advocate Deepak Chopra, "An intention is a directed impulse of consciousness that contains the seed form of that which you aim to create."[2]

Intentions are different from goals. Goals are specific things you want to achieve in the future. Intentions are guiding principles that you embrace and aim to embody in the present. They are more about the journey than the destination.

While the vision you set for yourself in the first section of this chapter is your motivator and the outcome you desire in undertaking this inner work, intentions are going to serve as the compass that helps you navigate your vulnerability journey.

At the end of the day, vulnerability is about being human. It's an emotional state triggered by the fact that you are a social being with interpersonal dealings. And when you deal with people, context matters. For example, how do you decide that it's safe to be vulnerable with someone? Opening up to a toxic coworker who bullies you at work isn't always the best idea. Or how do you deal with the lump in your throat and the cold sweats you feel when you want to share your feelings and needs with your partner? You may know that it's necessary for your relationship, but you still struggle to do it.

The truth is, there is no vulnerability roadmap. And that's why having a compass—your intentions—is more beneficial than aiming to have a step-by-step map for being vulnerable. Such a map doesn't exist. That said, every chapter of this workbook will help you deepen your understanding of vulnerability so that you'll be able to apply it beneficially in different contexts and know how to answer such questions as those posed above. You'll learn to feel confident about when it's safe to open up, and you'll know how to deal with the discomfort of being vulnerable when it becomes necessary.

While there's no roadmap, setting intentions at the beginning of your journey is important. This will help you arm yourself with guiding principles to follow from this moment onward, while walking toward your vision and learning about vulnerability.

If you have a college degree, are currently in school, or have ever taken up a hobby that required you to attend classes or workshops to learn a new skill, you might have unknowingly set intentions for that learning experience: avoid procrastination, be organized with your notes, make new friends, have fun, and so on. Those intentions guided your focus and actions. Perhaps you let yourself be goofy in dance class because your intention was to enjoy yourself, not to become a professional dancer. Maybe

---

2 Deepak Chopra, "5 Steps to Setting Powerful Intentions," Chopra.com, July 1, 2020. https://chopra.com /articles/5-steps-to-setting-powerful-intentions.

you declined party invites in order to finish an important paper instead of leaving it to the last minute because you had the intention of not procrastinating. Or you joined a student organization to meet new people because making friends in college was one of your intentions.

Now that you've wrapped your head around the idea of setting intentions and how it applies to your vulnerability journey, let's get started.

Intentions about Your Learning Experience

1. How do you want to approach this workbook? For example, you may want to aim to keep an open mind. Or you may decide that you will set time aside every week to complete the exercises. Define how you will make the most of your learning experience.

....

....

2. What will be your main focus?

....

....

3. What is the mindset you want to cultivate while working on embracing vulnerability?

....

....

4. How would you like to deal with moments when you feel a bit stuck?

....

....

Intentions about Your Relationship with Yourself

1. What are your expectations of yourself while doing this work?

....

....

THE **VULNERABILITY** WORKBOOK

2. In what ways will you be kind to yourself while doing this work?

3. How do you want to approach moments of discomfort?

4. How do you want to approach moments of self-doubt?

Intentions about How You Want to Show Up with Others

1. How do you intend to lead?

2. How do you intend to love?

3. How do you intend to communicate?

4. How do you intend to listen?

5. How do you intend to approach conversations?

....

....

6. What about difficult conversations and conflicts?

....

....

7. What about moments when others do or say something that isn't okay with you?

....

....

Narrowing Down Your Intentions

1. Review your answers to the previous questions. Do you notice any common themes? Group your answers around similar themes—communication, for instance, or open-mindedness.

....

....

2. If you had to choose a few core words—such as kindness, compassion, courage—to sum up the intentions you've listed, what would they be?

....

....

3. Make a list of three core intentions (one sentence each) that you want to carry with you on your vulnerability journey. "I will communicate even when it's hard" or "I will be kind to others and myself" are a couple of examples you can use for inspiration.

....

....

4. Why is each of these intentions important to you?

....

....

5. How will you remember your intentions? For example, you might want to print them out and put them on your bathroom mirror as a visual cue. Or you might want to set daily reminders on your phone.

....

....

Take Your Vision and Intentions with You

Congratulations—you now have a clear vision and intentions for your vulnerability journey! You have answered the call to adventure, and you feel the pull of your desired outcome. You have a good idea of how you want to show up while reading this workbook and completing the exercises in it. And you know what to keep in mind when you connect with yourself and interact with others. With a strong sense of purpose and a compass in your pocket, it's time now to venture further out.

Chapter 2

CULTIVATING SELF-AWARENESS

Self-awareness is ironic. Most people like to think they are self-aware. Yet we all lack awareness in some areas of our lives and psyches. And since we don't know what we don't know, it's hard to identify those blind spots.

To go from ignorance to awareness, you need tools that will help you observe your thoughts, feelings, and actions and expand the limits of your current level of consciousness. The goal is to use these insights to transform your life—noticing recurring patterns of behavior, for instance, and choosing to create new ones. Enter such resources as therapy and counseling, where a therapist can act like a mirror of sorts to help you gain greater self-awareness and inform positive change.

Wondering what this has to do with vulnerability? Well, pretty much everything. If you're reading this, you have some degree of self-awareness about your current capacity to be vulnerable and how that's affecting you. You also have some understanding of the way more vulnerability could impact your life for the better. This is a great start. But to cultivate vulnerability in a constructive way, you're going to have to develop more self-awareness. What got you here isn't what's going to get you to the vision that you fleshed out in Chapter 1. That pesky inner dialogue that tells you that people are going to reject you or judge you? Taming that requires self-awareness. The butterflies that show up in your stomach just as you're about to have a difficult conversation and share your true feelings? Those aren't going to be managed without—you guessed it—self-awareness.

In this chapter you will learn more about the state of being self-aware and why it's important for vulnerability. You will discover some of your blind spots when it comes to your relationship with yourself and others, and you'll explore some of your unconscious fears around vulnerability. You will learn how to develop greater self-awareness in your everyday life and then use that as a tool to increase your well-being and your ability to be vulnerable.

What Is Self-Awareness?

"Self-awareness is the ability to focus on yourself and how your actions, thoughts, or emotions do or don't align with your internal standards," according to psychologists Shelley Duval and Robert Wicklund, who developed self-awareness theory. "If you're highly self-aware, you can objectively evaluate yourself, manage your emotions, align your behavior with your values, and understand correctly how others perceive you."[3]

Dr. Tasha Eurich, an organizational psychologist and executive coach who conducted a large-scale study on self-awareness, identifies two types of self-awareness: internal and external self-awareness.[4] Internal self-awareness, says Eurich, is about clearly seeing yourself. What are your values? How do you fit into your environment? What are your strengths and weaknesses? How and why do you act and react—including your thoughts, feelings, and behaviors—and how do you impact others? Internal self-awareness is a form of introspection.

External self-awareness, on the other hand, is about your understanding of how others perceive you, around the same factors listed above for internal self-awareness. External self-awareness is a form of social cognizance.

Having high internal and external self-awareness has both benefits and downsides. Being in tune with yourself and reflecting on your internal state is useful for your personal growth. But according to author Meredith Betz in a BetterUp article, it can also veer into self-consciousness territory[5] and prevent you from sharing your true self with others. Being in tune with the way others perceive you can translate into well-developed social intelligence, but it can also make you overly concerned about the judgment of others, says Betz, and turn into inauthentic people-pleasing tendencies. So you want to aim for self-awareness, not self-consciousness.

Why Is Self-Awareness Important When It Comes to Vulnerability?

You may have different degrees of internal and external self-awareness. Regardless of where you fall on that spectrum, at this point on your journey it's important to know two things. First, self-awareness can be developed. This matters, because to get better at anything, you have to believe in your ability to

---

3 Shelley Duval and Robert A. Wicklund, *A Theory of Objective Self Awareness* (New York: Academic Press, 1972).

4 Tasha Eurich, "What Self-Awareness Really Is (and How to Cultivate It)," *Harvard Business Review,* January 4, 2018. https://hbr.org/2018/01/what-self-awareness-really-is-and-how-to-cultivate-it.

5 Meredith Betz, "Why Self-Awareness Is the Key Skill for Growth, Health, and Happiness," BetterUp, April 21, 2021. https://www.betterup.com/blog/what-is-self-awareness.

improve. Second, improving both internal and external self-awareness can help you flourish on your vulnerability journey and in life.

While studying self-awareness for the purpose of improving leadership skills, Eurich mapped out four self-awareness archetypes based on internal self-awareness (how well you know yourself) compared to external self-awareness (how well you understand the way others perceive you). People with both high internal and external self-awareness, according to Eurich, "know who they are, what they want to accomplish, and seek out and value others' opinions."

"This is where leaders begin to fully realize the true benefits of self-awareness," she adds. But replace leaders with any human being and you can quickly see how this applies to life in general, to relationships, and to vulnerability as well.

Knowing who you are and what you want to accomplish makes you feel more secure about sharing yourself with the world, even in the face of conflict. It helps you tolerate the risk of failure when you get out of your comfort zone to pursue your goals and desires, because you trust that you'll bounce back and keep moving forward when setbacks happen.

As for seeking out and valuing the opinions of others, that's also a huge piece of vulnerability. For example, asking for constructive feedback instead of being overly sensitive to criticism is a vulnerable thing to do. When you are able to hear and hold perspectives different from your own, others are able to feel safer about being vulnerable with you.

Self-awareness is clearly a central piece of the vulnerability puzzle. So let's further deconstruct the role it plays in your ability to be vulnerable, or your fear of doing so.

Exploring Your Vulnerability Blind Spots

The following self-reflection exercise will help you objectively assess your current thoughts, feelings, and actions. How do they affect your willingness and ability to be vulnerable?

When engaging in this kind of introspection, refrain from being hard on yourself or labeling things as "good" or "bad." Think of yourself as a gentle observer. You are there to observe and take notes on what you're seeing—not to beat yourself up. Yes, you might discover beliefs and patterns of behavior that have held you back without your even realizing it. But the beauty of self-awareness is that when you become conscious of something that has been holding you back, you can start to choose different ways of thinking, being, and acting.

It's important to keep this gentleness toward yourself in mind (you'll learn more in Chapter 3, about shame), because judging yourself harshly and feeling ashamed will only slow you down on your vulnerability journey. You are not uncovering blind spots to make yourself feel bad, but to use such insights in a constructive way.

REFLECTION

Complete the following sentences. Don't overthink your answers—go with your gut instincts, and keep going until you have nothing else to write.

1. Being vulnerable is scary because:

....

....

....

....

....

2. Being vulnerable sometimes makes me feel:

....

....

....

....

....

3. I feel unsafe expressing my true self and feelings when:

....

....

....

....

....

4. I am secretly afraid others will think:

....

....

....

....

....

5. The worst possible outcome of being vulnerable would be:

....

....

....

....

....

6. If this outcome happened, it would mean:

7. I currently handle my fears by:

8. I react to conflict by:

9. When people cross my boundaries, I react by:

_____

_____

_____

_____

_____

10. When my needs are not met, I tend to:

_____

_____

_____

_____

_____

11. My relationships are (sometimes difficult, satisfying but superficial, etc.):

_____

_____

_____

_____

_____

THE VULNERABILITY WORKBOOK

12. Other people are often (not to be trusted, more confident than me, etc.):

13. When I feel intense or difficult emotions, I tend to:

14. Communication is easy when:

15. Communication is challenging when:

....

....

....

....

....

Self-Awareness and Vulnerability in Everyday Life

Concepts such as self-awareness and vulnerability can seem abstract. In this section you'll see case studies of self-aware people who interact and use their awareness to demonstrate vulnerability along with examples that show a lack of self-awareness and a resulting destructive impact on vulnerability.

You'll then analyze each case study to refine your understanding of the relationship between self-awareness and vulnerability. It's always easier to observe things with objectivity when you're not personally involved, so let these case studies help fine-tune your sense of awareness before you turn your attention inward again.

CASE STUDY 1

Lauren takes care of people...a lot. From planning the perfect baby shower for her best friend to cleaning up after her roommate, taking charge and taking care of her loved ones comes naturally to her. Except that she is starting to feel worn out and resentful. It would be nice to be on the receiving end of thoughtful gestures, too, but her friends and family seem to take her for granted.

However, she swallows her negative feelings. For one thing, it would be awkward to share them. And she is a considerate person. Why shouldn't people treat her with consideration without her needing to say anything? Shouldn't it be a given?

One Friday evening, Lauren's best friend, Kayla, texts her and cancels their dinner plans at the last minute. Lauren replies, "Wow...OK. I'd already gotten ready, but I guess I'll just change and watch Netflix. I'll see you next week, then."

1. Lauren is aware that she is starting to feel resentful about doing so much for her loved ones. And she is aware that some of her emotional needs aren't being met in her close relationships. But she chooses to swallow her feelings. In what ways could she have used that awareness to show vulnerability instead?

2. How do you think this could have affected the outcome when Kayla canceled on her at the last minute?

3. Why does Lauren's reply to Kayla show a lack of self-awareness?

4. What do you think she felt when Kayla canceled?

....

....

....

....

5. What could Lauren have replied if she was aware of herself in that moment and allowed herself to be vulnerable?

....

....

....

....

CASE STUDY 2

Eddie has just picked up his boyfriend, Adam, to go on a date. While driving to the theater, Eddie notices that Adam seems quieter than usual, and moody. He asks him what's wrong. "Nothing," Adam says. "I can tell there's something wrong," insists Eddie.

Adam confesses that the night before, he noticed that Eddie had received a text message from a man he had never mentioned before. He didn't mean to snoop, but the name popped up on the screen. He tells Eddie that he trusts him but feels insecure about it and a little bit jealous.

Eddie feels a pang of defensiveness. He recognizes that feeling. He was raised in an authoritarian household, where he always had to explain himself and had no privacy. He's also been single for years and is not used to considering how his actions may impact a partner. But he loves Adam and understands how that text message might have made him feel.

He thanks Adam for sharing and proceeds to reassure him. The man is a coworker who invited him to join a basketball league, and he'd be happy to introduce Adam to him to put him more at ease.

1. How did Eddie demonstrate both internal and external self-awareness?

2. How did he use this awareness to show vulnerability?

3. How did that benefit the dynamic of the relationship?

4. What about Adam? Was he self-aware and vulnerable?

5. How did that benefit the dynamic of the relationship?

6. How might someone less self-aware than Eddie have reacted when feeling defensive?

THE **VULNERABILITY** WORKBOOK

7. How would that have impacted the dynamic of the relationship?

....

....

....

....

CASE STUDY 3

Maya has just started taking art lessons. She enjoyed painting and drawing as a teenager, and now that she's in her forties, she longs to reconnect to her creativity. The classes are enjoyable.

But the teacher has just announced that next week's workshop will entail a critique group to encourage students to get different perspectives on their work and to practice sharing feedback on their classmates' work. It's a key part of the learning process.

Maya feels sick to her stomach just thinking about it. Never mind that she won art competitions in her youth, and that she's received very positive comments from her art class teacher so far. She can't shake off thoughts that she is going to look stupid, that others are going to tear down her painting, and that she is not cut out to be an artist. The following week she skips class instead of participating in the critique group.

1. How does Maya lack self-awareness when it comes to objectively assessing her skill set?

....

....

....

....

2. What do you think about Maya's insecurities? How are they getting in the way of her initial intention to reconnect with her creativity and her enjoyment of the class?

3. How could more self-awareness help Maya manage her insecurities and be more vulnerable?

4. How could more vulnerability serve Maya in the context of this art class and in life?

What Does Your Future Self Think, Feel, and Believe?

You can clearly see the impact that a lack of self-awareness has on vulnerability—as well as the benefits of being self-aware when it comes to vulnerability. So now let's gain further clarity as to the thoughts, beliefs, and behaviors you would like to embody as you move forward. Where are there gaps to bridge, and what thoughts, beliefs, and behaviors might serve you better? It's best to complete the following activity and reflection exercise back to back, so make sure you can set aside at least half an hour of uninterrupted time for this.

ACTIVITY

Think about the vision you set for yourself in Chapter 1. Imagine that you possess a magic wand that lets you instantly teleport yourself into your desired future. You are there now, and you can taste and feel the wonderful impact of your vulnerability journey. Close your eyes and visualize your life and relationships after you've embraced this inner work.

REFLECTION

Now answer the following questions from the perspective of your future self. Don't overthink your answers. Go with your gut instinct, and keep going until you have nothing else to write.

1. Now that I am no longer held back by my fear of vulnerability and I am living authentically and courageously, I believe that I am (able to communicate my needs, worthy of being heard, etc.):

....

....

....

....

....

2. I believe that others are (doing their best, not out to get me, etc.):

_____

_____

_____

_____

_____

3. I believe that the world is (sometimes scary but also full of beauty, a playground to explore, etc.):

_____

_____

_____

_____

_____

4. I feel (free, authentic, etc.):

_____

_____

_____

_____

_____

5. My relationships are (deeply satisfying, healthy and balanced, etc.):

....

....

....

....

6. Communication is (a way to get on the same page in relationships, sometimes uncomfortable but important, etc.):

....

....

....

....

7. I embrace habits such as (sharing my feelings, getting out of my comfort zone more often, etc.):

....

....

....

....

8. I look forward to (continuing to deepen my intimacy with my partner, expressing myself more boldly, etc.):

....

....

....

....

....

9. When I feel intense or difficult emotions I (use it as an opportunity to connect with myself, show myself compassion, etc.):

....

....

....

....

....

10. I handle my fears by (reminding myself that I am safe, asking for support, etc.):

....

....

....

....

....

THE **VULNERABILITY** WORKBOOK

11. I perceive failure as (an opportunity for growth, a sign that I am living to the fullest, etc.):

....

....

....

....

12. I now see vulnerability as (a beautiful practice, a way to improve my life and relationships, etc.):

....

....

....

....

13. I deal with conflict by (facing it head on, expressing my concerns, etc.):

....

....

....

....

14. When other people cross my boundaries, I (politely tell them it's not okay, avoid self-abandoning to please them, etc.):

....

....

....

....

15. When my needs are not being met, I (make sure to communicate, take a moment to reflect on what I want to change in that relationship, etc.):

....

....

....

....

Identifying and Reframing Unhelpful Patterns

Congratulations! Being honest with yourself isn't always easy or comfortable, and you should be celebrating yourself for being willing to do what many people shy away from. If it feels a little uncomfortable, remember your original vision and intentions and the reason you began this journey in the first place. There will be rewards.

Let's keep digging so that you can start identifying and reframing any patterns that aren't serving you. Remember, you are developing self-awareness in order to uncover insights and drive positive transformation. You are getting to the most important part of this chapter's work.

1. What are some key differences between your current thoughts, beliefs, and behaviors and the ones from your ultimate vision?

2. Go through the answers you just wrote down about your current thoughts, beliefs, and behaviors. Do you notice any recurring themes?

3. Thinking of those themes, complete the following sentence:

I am afraid of being vulnerable because

and I believe that it could lead to

so it's causing me to

when I interact with others or put myself out there.

4. Is the previous sentence the absolute truth, as true as the existence of gravity? Can you find examples in your own life or in the world at large that challenge this perspective and show that it is not, in fact, an absolute truth?

....

....

....

....

....

5. What would you tell a best friend with similar beliefs? What kind of advice or words of comfort would you give?

....

....

....

....

....

6. Now go through the answers you wrote down in your ultimate vision about your future self's thoughts, beliefs, and behaviors. Do you notice any recurring themes?

....

....

....

....

....

7. Thinking of these themes, complete the following sentence:

In my vision, I embrace vulnerability because ....

.... and I believe that it could lead to ....

.... so I embrace habits and principles such as ....

.... when I interact with others or put myself out there.

8. Do you feel any resistance when reading the previous sentence? For example, you might notice frustration or skepticism. Don't judge yourself—just observe.

....

....

....

....

....

9. Where is that resistance coming from? Do you believe that it's possible for you to get to the place where you want to be with vulnerability? Do any fears or doubts come up in your mind? Perhaps the idea of embracing vulnerability raises the fear of getting hurt. Or maybe you feel discouraged because getting there feels like a huge challenge. Gently observe and write down what comes to mind, without labeling it as good or bad. For example, you might write, "I am afraid that being vulnerable will mean getting hurt."

....

....

....

....

....

10. Are these fears and doubts the absolute truth, as true as the existence of gravity? In the previous example, you might say, "It's true that I might get hurt by being vulnerable, but that doesn't mean that will always be the case—and never opening up or taking any risks will hurt me more in the long run."

....

....

....

....

11. Can you find examples in your own life or in the world that challenge your fears and doubts? Perhaps you have a positive memory about someone being vulnerable and not getting hurt. Maybe you saw your best friend fall in love and observed how vulnerable she was in the process, and how wonderful her relationship is now.

....

....

....

....

12. What would you tell a best friend about your fears and doubts?

....

....

....

....

13. What are some new thoughts you can get behind that feel somewhere between the thoughts and behaviors in your vision and the ones you have right now? Perhaps you don't quite believe that being vulnerable will be easy for you, but maybe a thought such as this feels believable: "Every day I choose to put myself out there a little more, and I know that it's going to pay off."

Putting New Patterns into Practice

Self-reflection is key for gaining greater self-awareness, whether it is guided by tools such as the journaling prompts you've just worked through, working with a professional, or simply spending time alone.

But transformation isn't only about reflecting. It's also about what you do daily and how you implement your newfound insights. Once you're aware of patterns that aren't serving you well and new ones you'd like to adopt, it's important to consistently observe your thoughts, feelings, and actions and adjust them accordingly until new patterns come naturally. And the more you do this, the more self-aware you will become.

This section will give you practical steps to incorporate into your life for greater self-awareness and positive vulnerability.

1. In light of your answers in the self-reflection exercises earlier in this chapter, what are some steps you can take right now to support your desired thoughts, feelings, and behaviors? Maybe you identified that you shy away from sharing honest feelings because you're afraid of being a burden. If that's the case, make it a point to notice every time you hold back from sharing your honest feelings, and get out of your comfort zone by expressing how you truly feel. Or perhaps you realized that you don't pursue goals or activities that you'd like to because you're afraid of failing or worried about what people will think if you do. One of your actions could be to choose one small goal that scares you and go after it.

ACTION STEP 1: ....

ACTION STEP 2: ....

ACTION STEP 3: ....

2. Remember your original vision and the thoughts, feelings, and behaviors of your future self in that vision? Choose three habits that your future self would approve of and embody. Incorporate at least one of them into your permanent routine. From choosing to feel your emotions even when they make you uncomfortable to seeking feedback from others instead of shying away from it, these could be any actions that will help you feel like your future self in the present moment.

HABIT 1: ....

HABIT 2: ....

HABIT 3: ....

3. Keep a daily log. Every evening, take a few minutes to look back on the day and identify three things that went well, three things that didn't go so well, and what you would do differently next time. Whether you're taking note of an interaction that left you feeling stressed-out or a moment that you're proud of, you'll strengthen your self-awareness muscles with this debriefing exercise.

Chapter 3

BUILDING SHAME RESILIENCE

In Chapter 2 you did some deep inner work. That was the first hurdle on your hero's journey toward embracing vulnerability and living a full, authentic, and courageous life that includes nourishing relationships. Some patterns you encountered were scary creatures blocking your way forward. But you were able to subdue them by working to reframe patterns and bridge the gap between your current state of consciousness and the one you desire.

You overcame one hurdle. But those unhelpful patterns have probably been automatic for years, if not for your whole life. Winning this first battle by using self-awareness is a great start, but it's normal for those pesky metaphorical beasts to rear their heads again. Instead of trying to kill them, aim to turn them into cute pets that no longer have so much power over your life. They'll continue to show up occasionally, especially as you get out of your comfort zone, so be prepared—but you'll learn to appease them and keep acting in alignment with your big vision.

You tamed them through the power of self-awareness, and now you are going to add another tool to your arsenal to continue this work: shame resilience. Shame resilience is a concept coined by Brené Brown, a researcher, lecturer, professor, and author known for her work on vulnerability.

Before diving further into what shame resilience is, it's important to understand shame itself. There's a reason you've held on to views of yourself, others, and the world, and to patterns of behavior that haven't served you well. It's a bit of a paradox. Technically, these patterns have indeed served you. They have worked hard to protect you and keep you safe from feeling shame.

So it is paramount to become familiar with the complex and universal human emotion of shame in order to continue this journey. It's normal to fear and avoid things you don't understand. It's also completely understandable to have built clever coping mechanisms allowing you to stay as far away from shame as possible. Taking a closer look will help you to break the cycle of unhelpful patterns you've resorted to in the past and solidify your new, desired patterns—the ones that align with your ultimate vision.

In this chapter you will learn more about shame and how it relates to vulnerability. And you will develop shame resilience skills to help you face your fear of vulnerability and start living beyond shame avoidance.

What Is Shame?

According to Brené Brown, shame is "the intensely painful feeling or experience of believing that we are flawed and therefore unworthy of love and belonging—something we've experienced, done, or failed to do makes us unworthy of connection."[6]

Connection is a fundamental human need. And shame is a universal human emotion that moves us away from it. For Brown, it's basically the enemy of connection and authenticity. And vulnerability, which means facing your shame, is the bridge to experiencing true connection and authenticity. Your fears around vulnerability and all the unhelpful patterns they have created in your life have protected you from feeling shame. They've been effective for that purpose—but at the cost of true connection and enjoying life as your true self. Unraveling this paradox is the next hurdle on your journey.

The first thing you need to know is that because shame makes us feel so icky, we shy away from even discussing it. So if you're struggling with feelings of shame, you might feel alone in your experience, but that couldn't be further from the truth.

Shame serves an evolutionary purpose—hence its universality. It's an emotion that regulates our behavior so we can avoid social ostracization and rejection, which used to be the equivalent of certain death. We survived as a species by sticking together in groups.

Shame vs. Guilt

If shame plays a necessary role in social inclusion, why can it make us feel so isolated? The answer lies in the difference between shame and guilt.

Brown says that guilt is a productive emotion. "I believe that guilt is adaptive and helpful—it's holding something we've done or failed to do up against our values and feeling psychological discomfort," she writes. "I don't believe shame is helpful or productive. In fact, I think shame is much more likely to be

---

6 Brené Brown, "Shame vs. Guilt," brenebrown.com, January 15, 2013. https://brenebrown.com/articles/2013 /01/15/shame-v-guilt.

the source of destructive, hurtful behavior than the solution or cure. I think the fear of disconnection can make us dangerous."[7]

Guilt is something you feel in relation to an action you've taken. It can encourage you to grow from your mistakes. Shame, on the other hand, is something you feel in relation to yourself and your identity. Think "I did something bad" versus "I am a bad person."

Shame holds you back from growth. It makes you internalize the sense of being flawed and unworthy of love, a self-fulfilling prophecy that then informs your actions. You'll be less likely to seek connection, less likely to face your fears of vulnerability in the pursuit of positive transformation, and more likely to isolate yourself. This might mean avoiding setting goals, entertaining harmful relationships because you don't think you're worthy of being treated well, or even harming others. You know what they say: "Hurt people hurt people." Shame can breed negative coping mechanisms to distract yourself from your feelings and numb them—such as substance abuse, overeating, or excessive online shopping.

Shame can also make you prone to overcompensation, another form of protecting yourself and running away from vulnerability. Like high-functioning addicts, those who overcompensate for their sense of shame may appear on the outside to have pretty good lives. Have you ever met someone with a huge ego who loves to name-drop, flaunt their wealth, or yield power and you thought to yourself, that person must be so insecure? That's another example of what internalized shame can do.

Shame takes on these dysfunctional forms when it spirals into toxic shame. It is no longer simply the emotion of shame. It lingers long after a specific behavior or situation you may have felt ashamed about and seeps into your day-to-day inner talk, as Crystal Raypole discusses on the Healthline website.[8] And many, many people walk through life without even knowing that their whole world is informed by the deeply rooted sense of shame they carry everywhere yet are simultaneously running away from.

If you recognize yourself in any of the previous examples, you may now feel ashamed about feeling shame. This is counterproductive and only perpetuates the cycle of shame and disconnection. So what now?

Shame Resilience: What Is It and Why Does It Matter?

Enter shame resilience, the key to embracing vulnerability in the face of shame, according to Brené Brown. Shame resilience is a set of skills to help you face shame, feel it, speak about it, and move through it authentically. The result? More courage and connection than if you had avoided it.

---

7 Brené Brown. https://brenebrown.com/articles/2013/01/15/shame-v-guilt.
8 Crystal Raypole, "Where Toxic Shame: Comes From and How to Work Through It," Healthline, September 23, 2020. https://www.healthline.com/health/mental-health/toxic-shame#causes.

In her research, Brown has identified four elements of practicing shame resilience:[9]

1. Recognizing shame and understanding its triggers. This is about knowing that you're experiencing shame, naming it, and taking the time to feel it and understand what triggered it. Understanding your shame triggers is the first step to coping with them constructively.

2. Practicing critical awareness. Practicing critical awareness is about acknowledging why shame exists, what it is, and how it affects you and others. This allows you to keep things in perspective. You're not the first or the last person to feel this way.

3. Reaching out. Reaching out and sharing your shame story with people you trust allows you to experience empathy and feel connected to others.

4. Speaking shame. Speaking about your shame even though you are tempted to hide it is important in order to combat its negative effects. Shame thrives on secrecy and diminishes when you find the courage to speak up.

The Importance of Building Shame Resilience

Why is building shame resilience so important? If you don't recognize shame, don't practice critical awareness, and avoid reaching out and speaking about your shame, you end up embracing unhelpful reactions to shame as a defense mechanism.

As in some of the examples previously mentioned and some of the personal examples you may have uncovered in Chapter 2, unhelpful shame responses all have one thing in common. They reject vulnerability and disconnect you from yourself and from others.

---

9 Brené Brown, "Shame Resilience Theory: A Grounded Theory Study on Women and Shame," in *Families in Society: The Journal of Contemporary Social Services 87*, no. 1 (2006): 43–52. https://doi.org/10.1606/1044 -3894.3483.

REFLECTION

1. What are your top shame triggers? For example, maybe you feel shame when you make a mistake or get negative feedback. Or perhaps you are terrified of people judging you.

2. What are your go-to unhelpful shame responses? As an example, you may be overly agreeable and try to be liked by everyone to avoid being judged.

3. Moving forward, what can you do when shame is triggered? Maybe you'll decide to be kind to yourself when you notice your shame. Perhaps you'll reach out to a trusted friend to talk about it, or you'll write down your feelings in your journal.

....

....

....

....

....

***

Shame and Shame Resilience in Action

Take a break from exploring how shame shows up for you by analyzing how it can affect different people in different situations. This awareness will not only help you become more astute about the concept of shame and how it pertains to vulnerability, but it will also help you feel more compassion for yourself for experiencing something so universal.

CASE STUDY 1

Priya has just started a new job. Her colleagues are quite friendly and often socialize outside of work. They've already invited her to join happy hour twice, and she's declined both times, giving an excuse. She gets stressed-out about social events, especially with people at work. But the next event will actually be during work hours, a daytime bowling activity to celebrate a coworker's birthday. Her boss is going to be there, too, and she feels that it would look kind of bad to skip the event.

The night before the event, Priya feels anxious, plagued by thoughts of being really bad at bowling in front of others. At the event, she downs her first drink really fast and starts to feel herself loosen up. She ends up doing okay at bowling—some hits and misses. She bonds with a couple of coworkers and, three drinks in, starts sharing more of her personal opinions. In conversation, Priya reveals that she thinks a certain popular TV show is terrible. One of her coworkers responds that it's her favorite show.

Priya apologizes, but the coworker brushes it off and jokes about it. The conversation moves on, but the next morning Priya wakes up with a sense of dread.

She can't stop obsessing about her bowling performance and feeling embarrassed about the shots she missed. She feels ashamed about having had three drinks and wonders if she looked stupid. And she feels terrible about her TV show comment—what if that coworker was offended? At the office, she stays away from that coworker. In fact, she stays away from most people and can't wait for the day to end so she can go back home.

1. How does Priya's shame manifest itself in social situations with her coworkers?

2. What are Priya's responses to her shame? How do they inform her actions?

3. How is Priya avoiding vulnerability and creating greater disconnection?

4. How could Priya have used shame resilience skills to cope?

5. How might that benefit her relationship with herself and her coworkers?

6. How could shame resilience improve her life and sense of well-being?

CASE STUDY 2

Isaac has always struggled to feel confident with women. He has watched some of his friends have casual flings or build meaningful long-term relationships with great partners and has secretly envied their confidence, success, good looks, or sense of humor. He has recently met Emily, a woman he really likes. They've been seeing each other regularly for a couple of month and get along really well, and she says she likes him a lot.

But Isaac can't shake the feeling that Emily is going to leave him and that it's only a matter of time before she discovers that she would rather be with someone else. Even though Isaac and Emily have agreed to date exclusively and delete dating apps from their phones, he downloads Tinder again. Emily has no idea that he's done this, but he is now talking to a few other women while continuing his relationship with her.

1. How is Isaac's shame manifested in his inner talk?

2. How is Isaac's shame manifested in his dating life?

....

....

....

....

3. What are Isaac's responses to his shame? How do they inform his actions?

....

....

....

....

4. How is Isaac avoiding vulnerability and creating more disconnection?

....

....

....

....

5. How could Isaac have used shame resilience skills to cope?

....

....

....

....

6. How would that benefit his relationship with himself and with Emily?

....

....

....

....

7. How could shame resilience improve his life and his sense of well-being?

....

....

....

....

Camila has signed up for a running event to benefit breast cancer research. She has been promoting the event for a few weeks on social media and has asked some of her friends and family to donate money for the cause. Camila has now raised hundreds of dollars, but she feels increasing anxiety about the upcoming race.

The truth is, she hasn't started training and keeps procrastinating on following her running plan. She initially thought that signing up for the event would be a great way to stay committed to her fitness goals. But now the run is only a couple of weeks away, and she hasn't trained at all. She doesn't think she can do it, but she feels disappointed in herself and is afraid that she will disappoint everyone who donated money for her fundraiser. That thought makes her feel deep shame, and she starts to cry.

She realizes that she is feeling shame and calls her sister, Valentina, to confess. Valentina listens with empathy and tells her that she understands. She suggests that Camila reach out individually to everyone who donated money to be honest about the situation and say how bad she feels about it. Camila follows her advice, and most people are understanding. They are not mad at her, and they don't mind having donated money to a good cause.

1. How does Camila's shame manifest itself?

2. How does Camila effectively use shame resilience skills?

3. How did courage and vulnerability help Camila?

4. How did shame resilience help Camila move toward connection and authenticity?

5. What could have happened if Camila had resorted to unhelpful coping mechanisms in response to her shame?

6. How might that have worsened the situation?

How to Deal with Shame and Develop Shame Resilience

You now have both greater self-awareness and a better understanding of shame and the role it plays in your vulnerability journey. Reflect on how shame shows up for you, how you respond, and how shame resilience can help you move through your shame with greater courage, vulnerability, authenticity, and connection.

1. What are some "aha" moments about how shame shows up in your life and how you tend to respond to it?

2. Reflect on a time when you felt shame and had an unhelpful response to it. What happened? How did you feel? What did you do? What kind of consequences did your actions have?

3. Reflect on a time when you felt shame and effectively used shame resilience skills. What happened? How did you feel? What did you do? What kind of consequences did your actions have?

4. In what ways are your personal shame feelings universal? Can you think of other people who may be feeling just like you do but aren't speaking up about it?

5. How does your shame show up in your inner talk? What thoughts do you have about yourself on a daily basis?

....

....

....

....

6. What consequences do those thoughts have on your life?

....

....

....

....

7. Moving forward, how can you use self-awareness and shame resilience to manage those thoughts more effectively?

....

....

....

....

THE **VULNERABILITY** WORKBOOK

8. How will that benefit your life and well-being?

....

....

....

....

Putting Shame Resilience Skills into Practice

Now that you've developed greater insight about your shame-related tendencies and how you can manage them in more constructive ways, it's time to put that learning into practice.

1. In light of your answers in the self-reflection exercises earlier in this chapter, what steps can you take right now to manage your shame by using shame resilience instead of unhelpful patterns that shield you from vulnerability? For example, maybe you've recognized that you are ashamed about having gained weight and don't feel worthy of a romantic relationship until you've lost weight. You've been avoiding dating. But now you recognize your shame and decide to speak about it with a trusted friend. Experiencing and voicing your shame while feeling a friend's support helps you feel braver and more connected. As a result, you realize that you are worthy of love at any weight and download a dating app.

ACTION STEP 1: ....

....

ACTION STEP 2: ....

....

ACTION STEP 3: ....

....

2. Choose three habits that can help combat your shame triggers through shame resilience skills, then incorporate at least one of them in your life on a permanent basis. Perhaps you've experienced feelings of shame in social settings and tend to cope by drinking too much. You decide that you will have one glass of water for every drink when attending social events and will limit your overall alcohol consumption for the evening. And you'll choose at least one friendly face to engage with authentically, sharing your true thoughts without performing or "being on."

HABIT 1: ....

....

HABIT 2: ....

....

HABIT 3: ....

....

3. Form a support network of friends that you can share your shame story with and reach out to when you feel triggered. Make a list of people in your life that you trust, or online support groups that resonate with you. Make it a point to reach out and share your shame story at least once while you are completing this workbook.

Possible people and groups:

....

....

....

....

....

....

THE **VULNERABILITY** WORKBOOK

Chapter 4
PRACTICING AUTHENTIC COMMUNICATION

The first chapters of this workbook have taken you on an inward journey—and there's a reason for that. The deeper your relationship with yourself, the deeper your relationships with others can be. Without pausing to think about the inner workings of your mind and feelings, you would be at the mercy of external circumstances. You would react to situations without being conscious of all the factors at play that prevent you from being vulnerable and negatively affect your relationships and your life.

But now you have greater awareness. You have identified some unhelpful patterns to unlearn on your quest to embrace vulnerability. And you have also learned about a universal yet rarely discussed vulnerability obstacle: shame, and all the ways you avoid it to protect yourself while inadvertently moving away from connection.

You have started turning these insights into vulnerability-embracing actions. And perhaps you've even experienced some of the benefits of being intentional about cultivating vulnerability while developing self-awareness and shame resilience. It's time to keep building on what you have explored so far by turning your focus outward a bit more. Enter communication—specifically, authentic communication, which can only happen with vulnerability.

Something happens when you identify your fears of vulnerability, understand how they are trying to protect you in a counterproductive way, and start doing things differently. The way you communicate changes. It's inevitable. For example, if you are self-aware enough to realize that you don't share your true feelings during moments of conflict because you fear rejection (and the sting of shame that comes with it), what will you do during the next conflict you encounter? Well, if you want to break the cycle of shame and embrace courage and vulnerability, the alternative is to express your true feelings instead of hiding them. This is how inner work translates into lasting change, one moment at a time, and how vulnerability plays out beyond the pages of your journal.

In this chapter you'll learn about authentic communication—what it is and the role it plays on your vulnerability journey. You will tie together self-awareness and shame resilience to develop your own authentic communication skills. And, of course, you will reap the benefits of authentic communication, which include more meaningful interactions and greater life satisfaction.

What Is Authentic Communication?

To understand the role that authentic communication plays in your vulnerability adventure, let's define authenticity first.

Authenticity is such a buzzword, but wrapping your head around what it looks like in practice—and in this case, during conversations—helps to truly get it and benefit from it. Terms like "genuine," "real," or "true" pop up in dictionary definitions of authenticity. So authentic communication is simply the idea of communicating in a genuine, real, and true manner.

But unless you are used to walking around being brutally honest and admitting that you hate someone's new haircut, chances are that as a socially conditioned human being you don't always say what you truly mean. And that's okay. Authentic communication isn't about being gratuitously inappropriate or rude.

What it *is* about is consistent alignment among thoughts, feelings, words, and actions. Because your actions send messages. It's who you are on the inside, consistently expressed on the outside. It's about being in tune with what you're thinking and feeling in a given moment and then speaking it. And if it were easy, everyone would do it.

But the opposite is often true. Gossip, people-pleasing, and passive-aggressive comments are common failures of authentic communication. Why? Because it takes vulnerability to communicate authentically. What if someone reacts negatively to your true thoughts and feelings? What if they judge you? What if they feel awkward and, in turn, you feel awkward as well? What if they misunderstand your true intentions?

There are many reasons for choosing to bypass authenticity and say things that don't reflect what's really going on within you. Not all of them are ill-intentioned. Many are rooted in the patterns explored in Chapter 2 and in the shame-avoidance uncovered in Chapter 3. But in bypassing authenticity, you also rob others of the choice to authentically engage and respond to your true thoughts and feelings. How can they do so if they aren't aware of what those thoughts and feelings are? Authentic communication is critical for meaningful connection—and it comes as a result of vulnerability.

REFLECTION

1. Identify three situations when you communicated authentically— maybe delivering honest feedback to a coworker or refusing to take part in something with which you just weren't comfortable. What happened? How did authentic communication affect the outcome? Why did you choose to communicate authentically?

2. Identify three situations in which you failed to communicate authentically, whether it was attending an event for people-pleasing reasons or lying to a romantic partner to avoid conflict. What happened? How did it affect the outcome of the situation? Why did you avoid authentic communication?

3. In light of your answers to the previous two questions, what are some patterns that show up for you around authentic communication? When do you tend to communicate authentically and when do you tend to avoid doing so? Why?

....

....

....

....

....

....

Self-Awareness, Shame Resilience, and Authenticity

It's impossible for authentic communication to happen if you're not even aware of what you truly think and feel. Self-awareness is thus the first step to communicating authentically. What is true for you in a given moment? It gets a bit more complicated, though. Have you ever had trouble admitting some of your true feelings and thoughts to yourself? This is how shame resilience comes into play to facilitate authentic communication. Some of your genuine desires, opinions, fears, or concerns may bring up feelings of shame. And since shame feels so icky, it's easy to refuse to acknowledge the desires, opinions, fears, or concerns that bring it up, let alone say them out loud to other people.

This is called an inner conflict: two opposing driving forces within you. In this case, thoughts and feelings you genuinely hold are in conflict with beliefs about those thoughts and feelings that make you feel ashamed of them. Let's use a concrete example to illustrate this. A busy mother feels exhausted and overwhelmed. She longs for a full day to herself without kids, responsibilities, or obligations. But when her husband asks if she needs more help, she declines. She feels shame about her tiredness and desire to take time off, because she believes it makes her inadequate as a mom.

So being in tune with your inner world isn't only a matter of self-awareness—in this case, the mother is completely aware of how tired and overwhelmed she feels—but also requires shame resilience. With shame resilience, she could face her feelings of inadequacy and even express them to her husband while accepting his help. Using self-awareness and shame resilience lets you feel what you're feeling and think what you're thinking with greater clarity, and then speak it.

You may notice yourself wanting to hold back for one of the common reasons people avoid authentic communication. These include feeling worried about the other party's reaction, embarrassed about your opinions, or obligated to say a certain thing because of real or perceived social pressure. All of these reasons are rooted in avoiding unpleasant outcomes and emotions such as shame. They help you stay in control of a conversation's outcome and others' perception of you. But arming yourself with shame resilience gives you the courage to be vulnerable, because you know that if you do lose control of the interaction and end up experiencing shame, it won't be pleasant but you will be able to tolerate it. It's a way of facing your fears, not by denying that they can come true but by knowing that you will be okay if they do.

The truth is, you can't control how other people are going to react to your truth. They may judge or reject you. Therein lies the most vulnerable aspect of authentic communication. But with it comes a powerful form of freedom that makes it all worthwhile

Are you really free if your shame keeps you trapped and you don't express your true nature? If you don't get to experience the feeling of being loved, seen, understood, and accepted for who you truly are? If you care more about what people think than about betraying yourself? Facing your fears and letting go of control by practicing authentic communication liberates you from the shackles of living a repressed version of yourself. It's about saying "so what?" to the threat of shame and "yes" to love and life—as you are, perfectly imperfect, and yet so worthy of love, acceptance, and connection.

The best part is that in taking off your masks and pretenses, you give others permission to do the same—and they tend to appreciate it. They exhale a mental sigh of relief at the idea of not having to be "on." Nobody likes to be "on." You know the feeling, right? Small talk that nobody cares about yet everyone feels pressure to engage in. An elephant in the room around a topic no one is brave enough to touch.

On the other hand, authentic communication allows the elephant to be spoken of and the conversation to take incredibly honest and productive forms. It replaces vapid small talk with wonderfully human, wonderfully interesting discussions in which you get to know people better, with all their quirks and qualities. It finds common ground where there was none. It expands minds and creates solutions. It addresses relationship problems at their core and strengthens bonds. It is the only form of communication that truly matters, yet we run away from it in an attempt to ward off shame and live without vulnerability.

REFLECTION

1. How can you use self-awareness to increase your ability to communicate authentically? This might mean noticing when you're not expressing your true thoughts and feelings and pausing before responding.

2. How can you use shame resilience to increase your ability to communicate authentically? This might look like taking a moment to tune in with yourself when you are avoiding authentic communication and identifying what you are afraid of and how you're protecting yourself from shame, then soothing yourself through positive self-talk.

3. How is avoiding authentic communication negatively impacting your life? For example, you might be stuck in a relationship in which you feel deeply unhappy because you are afraid of the consequences of speaking up.

....

....

....

....

....

4. How will embracing authentic communication benefit you? Maybe you will feel less stressed out about your schedule once you stop saying yes to everything out of a sense of obligation.

....

....

....

....

....

Authentic vs. Inauthentic Communication

Wondering how to differentiate authentic and inauthentic communication? Analyze the case studies below to explore different scenarios in which people make the choice to communicate authentically or avoid authentic communication.

Krista is having dinner with her three best friends. As always, it's great to catch up and hear about everyone's life updates, from career challenges to wedding and travel plans. Krista has just started a new job at a big-name company that many people aspire to work for. Everyone congratulates her and is excited for her.

Later, her friend Yasmeen leans in and asks her if she could refer her for a role. Krista is uneasy with the idea—she has seen Yasmeen struggle with one job after another, always leaving a company on bad terms. And she doesn't feel comfortable mixing friendship with work. But as Yasmeen looks at her, smiling and waiting for an answer, she feels caught off guard. "Sure," she says. "Send me your resume."

1. How did Krista demonstrate self-awareness?

2. How did Krista fail to communicate authentically?

3. Why do you think she chose to communicate inauthentically despite being in tune with her true thoughts and feelings?

_____

_____

_____

_____

4. In what ways is she avoiding vulnerability by avoiding authenticity?

_____

_____

_____

_____

5. How could this affect her relationship with Yasmeen?

_____

_____

_____

_____

6. How could this affect her at work?

....

....

....

....

7. What could she have told Yasmeen instead?

....

....

....

....

8. Is it too late to communicate authentically? What could she do, moving forward, to rectify the situation and share her true thoughts and feelings with Yasmeen?

....

....

....

....

Niko is attending a conference for work. There are vendors and sponsors who want to meet potential clients to offer their solutions and products. Niko has met people wanting to sell him things all day long. They're just doing their jobs, of course, but he senses feigned interest in where he is from, what he does, and what he has to say. It's now cocktail hour, and he walks to the bar to grab a drink, hoping for a small reprieve from small talk. These events tend to zap his energy, but traveling for work is a great perk of his job and the conference is valuable as far as making new business connections.

As he waits for the bartender to serve his drink, a man walks up next to him and says, "God, if anyone else asks me about how my team is handling remote work and pitches me their software, I am going to head to my room until dinner." Niko laughs, tells him he agrees, and introduces himself.

The man's name is Anand, and he is the CEO of a fast-growing startup. He and his wife had recently had a baby, and it's the first time he has traveled away from home since his son's birth. It feels like a nice break, but he's also afraid of missing out—his wife sent him a video of his son taking his first steps while he was away. He shows the video to Niko, who finds Anand's genuineness refreshing and now feels inspired to open up.

He tells Anand about his passion for diving and how he's taking a couple of days off after the conference to go diving. He mentions that he's happy in his role but challenged because he is short-staffed. He has great strategic ideas but feels caught between putting out day-to-day fires at work and reaching higher-level goals. The conversation flows. The two men walk away exchanging contact information, and a few weeks later they connect over a business partnership opportunity that benefits both of them.

1. How did Anand's authenticity positively impact Niko?

2. How did Niko choose to engage in authentic communication when approached by Anand at the bar?

---

3. How were both Anand and Niko vulnerable in the context of this business setting?

---

4. What were some of the professional benefits of authentic communication between Anand and Niko?

THE VULNERABILITY WORKBOOK

5. Why are both Anand and Niko put off by the salespeople's communication style? How could the salespeople at the conference use authentic communication for better results?

....

....

....

....

....

CASE STUDY 3

Luna and Joel have been dating for a month and a half. They have been seeing each other a couple of times a week, getting to know each other through different activities. As yet they haven't had any conversations about their relationship, such as whether they are exclusive and where they see the relationship going.

They clearly like each other, but Luna's anxiety is growing, along with her feelings for Joel. She really likes him and doesn't want to see anyone else. In fact, she could see herself getting into a serious relationship with him. She is wondering if he feels the same. And she is worried that he might not be on the same page and just sees the relationship as a casual romance. He hasn't expressed explicit interest in things progressing any further, after all.

The next time she sees him, and even though she feels super anxious about having a "relationship talk," Luna tells Joel that she is not interested in dating other people. "Listen, I really like you, but I am not sure I am ready for a serious relationship. I'd like to keep seeing you and exploring how things go," he replies.

Luna notices a sinking feeling in her stomach. She does her best to smile and casually shares that she completely understands—that it makes sense, and she wants to keep seeing him and see how things go, too. Later that night, when he drops her at home, she cries from disappointment. But she tells herself that Joel might eventually commit to her. Besides, she is not ready to lose him.

1. How did Luna fail to communicate authentically?

2. Why is Luna afraid of being vulnerable?

3. How is Luna avoiding shame by not communicating authentically?

4. How could this affect her and her relationship with Joel in the long run?

5. What could Luna have done differently in response to Joel's feelings about their relationship?

6. How could Luna have used self-awareness and shame resilience to navigate this relationship situation with authentic communication?

7. Is it too late to communicate authentically? What could she do, moving forward, to rectify the situation and share her true thoughts and feelings with Joel?

....

....

....

....

....

Authentic Communication Strengths and Weaknesses

You can see that there are many different settings in which the opportunity for authentic communication presents itself. And there are also various reasons for avoiding authentic communication. Reflect on your own authentic communication strengths and weaknesses below so that you can improve your ability to freely express yourself.

1. What are your authentic communication strengths? For example, you may feel very comfortable communicating authentically in your romantic relationships.

....

....

....

....

....

2. How can you build on these strengths? For example, if you realize that expressing your needs in your romantic relationship comes easy, you can practice expressing your needs in other relationships, such as those with friends and family.

3. What are some areas of improvement you can focus on regarding authentic communication? Perhaps you feel guilty a lot, so you always put others first. Maybe you dread conflict and prefer not to speak your authentic truth for fear of ruffling feathers.

4. In what ways do you avoid vulnerability by avoiding authentic communication? For example, maybe you are afraid of being laughed at for being too sensitive when the time comes to express negative feelings.

Bringing Authenticity to Your Daily Conversations

Now it's time to bring authentic communication to your daily conversations. Practice makes perfect, and there will be plenty of moments when you notice yourself not communicating authentically. That's okay, and to be expected. As you develop greater self-awareness and greater shame resilience and you continue to build the habit of authentic communication, it will come more naturally in all areas of your life. Meanwhile, use any moments of inauthentic communication as learning opportunities.

1. Moving forward, is there an area of your life that requires more authentic communication? As an example, perhaps authentically communicating with your family feels challenging right now, but it's needed because you don't feel safe being yourself with them and avoid them as a result.

2. What is the next opportunity to put authentic communication into practice in the area of your life you've just identified?

....

....

ACTIVITY

1. Get into the habit of pausing before responding. Notice when you are tempted to avoid authentic communication in your daily conversations.

2. Use moments of inauthenticity as feedback. If you realize that you didn't share your true feelings and thoughts in a conversation, use that moment as an opportunity to understand why and to make a different choice the next time around.

Chapter 5

ESTABLISHING HEALTHY BOUNDARIES

As you practice authentic communication, you'll encounter your own personal boundaries. Yes, you're free next Thursday but no, you don't actually want to go to that event. No, you're not comfortable with your brother staying at your place for an entire month. Yes, you need extra time to work on that project.

You might have noticed that your thoughts and feelings evolve, too. You sometimes express what seems authentic to you in a given moment, then later change your mind and feel differently. At times when you are asked questions, you may feel that you have no answers. In those instances, "I don't know" may be the most authentic response.

All this is to be expected—and celebrated. Authenticity is human. Humans are full of paradoxes. They are continuously evolving. Your commitment to authentic communication is about expressing your truth at a given point in time and in a given context, knowing that it might change—and that if it does, you can reexpress yourself.

Mastering the art of communicating authentically also provides the perfect opportunity to learn how to establish healthy boundaries. Boundaries are expressed through authentic communication. In fact, they are a form of authentic communication, as they pertain to being honest about your thoughts and feelings. But they require some practice, since they can involve interpersonal negotiations in which you state your expectations about how you'd like others to interact with you.

In this chapter you will learn everything you need to know about setting boundaries: what boundaries are, why they matter, and how to establish healthy ones. You will be able to make use of all the vulnerability pillars you have implemented so far. You'll use self-awareness to be aware of your thoughts, feelings, and needs, authentically expressing them and setting boundaries as necessary. And you'll rely on shame resilience to navigate any discomfort that may arise in the process.

Bringing boundaries into your relationships will strengthen them. With clearly defined expectations, there will be more trust and less confusion. More straightforward communication and fewer assumptions. More respect and less give-and-take imbalance.

You will learn about the ways boundaries support relationships and protect you from relationships that are problematic. And in doing so, boundaries will help you feel even more confident about your ability to be vulnerable.

What Are Boundaries?

Boundaries are limits. They can be physical, mental, or emotional. They define what you are available for and what you will not tolerate, where your space starts and another person's demands or intrusion into that space need to end—whether they are well-meaning or not. Sometimes you must tell others about your boundaries; at other times it's not necessary, but you know they are there and act accordingly.

Boundaries can vary depending on the context. For example, there are professional boundaries. As a manager, you may be friendly and warm with your team but not cross the line of becoming close friends in order to avoid potential conflicts of interest. Or you may have boundaries around checking your emails after work hours.

Personal boundaries can look different in different relationships. Take close family members versus acquaintances. You may choose to hear the concerns of your parents about one of your decisions—which doesn't mean you'll change your mind to please them but that you'll be open to what they have to say—while being closed off to a casual acquaintance giving you unsolicited advice on the same topic. In a romantic relationship, you may not appreciate your partner unexpectedly coming home late without sending you a heads-up. Or you may value alone time in the morning while having coffee.

Some boundaries are nonnegotiable across the board—like not tolerating disrespect, whether it's from your boss, your dad, or a stranger on the street yelling and cursing at you.

Boundaries, at their core, are a simple concept. Again, they are limits—your chosen limits. But things get complex because other people have boundaries, too. When boundaries inevitably clash, it can lead to one of two outcomes. The first one, renegotiating the terms of an interaction or a relationship to create a win-win, is the best-case scenario with people you care about who are capable of having and respecting healthy boundaries (we'll get to what that means shortly). By discussing boundaries, you can gain a deeper understanding of each other and walk away with clearer guidelines for your relationship. The second outcome is perhaps less pleasant but sometimes necessary. When one person's needs trample another's and you can't renegotiate the interaction or relationship, you might need to disengage or even end the relationship in order to respect your boundaries.

To make matters more nuanced, sometimes you don't even know what your own limits are, so you're not choosing them consciously. If you've never learned how to set healthy boundaries, you can end up in a position in which you don't have enough limits or have limits that are too rigid. That's problematic when interacting with others. If you have no limits, you'll end up in imbalanced relationships in which your needs are disregarded. You might attract people into your life who will test your boundaries, sense that there are none, walk all over you, and wreak havoc in your life. If your limits are too rigid, on the other hand, you'll keep people at a distance and end up in imbalanced relationships. You'll have no room to compromise when it comes to the needs of others. You'll engage in surface-level relationships that don't require any flexibility on your end.

Are those scenarios conducive to meaningful connection and satisfying relationships? No. Healthy boundaries help create the conditions in which relationships can thrive. Think of it as being like a sports game. There are rules. Without the rules of the game, players would aimlessly roam around the field. Rules allow players to focus on playing the game and responding to what is happening in real time. In your relationships, boundaries are the rules of the game. Knowing that they are there, you can focus on engaging in your relationships in real time, using all the skills you are developing through this workbook. This sets the ground for constructive, secure vulnerability.

Since vulnerability is about emotional exposure, boundaries help you adjust your level of emotional exposure to what is healthy and safe. Vulnerability is not a free-for-all. You don't owe anyone your vulnerability. And you don't have to share all of yourself with everyone at all times. When you know that you have healthy boundaries, you can relax into opening up as much as you want, knowing that your boundaries can kick in when warranted—as in situations where someone is making you uncomfortable or causing you harm.

What Unhealthy Boundaries Look Like

It's easy to see how someone who has built walls all around themself is avoiding any emotional exposure. But those who have no boundaries and engage in one-sided relationships—where they give and give while others take and take—are overexposed. They are vulnerable in an unhealthy way, one that is harmful for them. And in another way, they are avoiding healthy vulnerability. They keep themselves busy by focusing on others' experience at the expense of their own. They are refusing to face their real thoughts, feelings, and needs—which may be scary and uncomfortable to acknowledge and feel and can require courage to express. And as you now know, it takes self-awareness and shame resilience to be deeply in tune with yourself. It also takes self-love.

Yes, setting boundaries is also an act of self-love. You love yourself, so you allow your experience and emotions to take up space. You love yourself, so you know that your needs matter. You love yourself, so you feel worthy of prioritizing yourself. You love yourself, and you cannot fathom the idea of engaging in dynamics that require you to abandon yourself. You love yourself, so you use your voice to tell others about your limits or to make requests, even when it's difficult or they don't react well.

You may be surprised to know that you can even experience unhealthy boundaries with yourself. Overindulging or overworking are perfect examples. Such weak boundaries with yourself are usually synonymous with a lack of self-love and vulnerability avoidance. Loving yourself means taking care of yourself—and going for a second bag of chips or working yourself until burnout is *not* a demonstration of self-care. Those things show an avoidance of vulnerability, because sitting with uncomfortable emotions is a more vulnerable state than drinking, eating, or working to escape them.

On the other hand, setting overly rigid boundaries with yourself can look like being a perfectionist or never letting loose. That can mean that you are avoiding the vulnerability of potentially making a mistake, and that you only love yourself when you meet self-imposed unrealistic standards—not when you're a human being who has flaws.

SELF-REFLECTION

Did you have any "aha" moments about the way boundaries manifest themselves in your life? Using the prompts below, take some time to explore your own boundaries as well as any areas you'd like to improve when it comes to setting healthy boundaries.

1. Identify three situations where you had healthy boundaries—such as refusing to take on extra responsibilities at work without receiving a pay raise, perhaps. What happened? How did your boundaries affect the outcome of the situation? Why did you choose to set these boundaries?

2. Identify three situations where you failed to have healthy boundaries—such as allowing a partner to disrespect you in arguments by tolerating his or her behavior. What happened? How did it affect the outcome of the situation? Why did you avoid setting boundaries?

....

....

....

....

....

....

3. In light of your answers to the previous two questions, what are some patterns that show up for you around boundaries? Where do you tend to struggle with boundaries, and why? For example, you might feel awkward setting boundaries when you feel it will offend others.

....

....

....

....

....

....

4. What can you focus on to set healthy boundaries with yourself and others? Perhaps you'll remove yourself from situations that make you feel uncomfortable, or you'll take a step back from a specific relationship or relationship dynamic.

5. In what ways do you avoid true vulnerability by having poor boundaries? For instance, perhaps you keep dating people who don't treat you well because you are afraid of intimacy.

The Dos and Don'ts of Setting Boundaries

Are you starting to connect more dots between your relationship with yourself and your relationships with others? Good, because setting boundaries starts with identifying what your boundaries are. There are three steps to setting a boundary:

1. Define the boundary. What are you okay with and not okay with? What do you want? What do you need? Check in with yourself. Your emotions can usually point you in the direction of your needs. For example, if you're feeling stressed about an invitation, you may be stretched thin and would rather decline so that you can rest.

2. Express the boundary. Focus on making statements about your needs without accusing, blaming, or criticizing anyone. "I don't feel comfortable with this" or "I need time for quiet work; I'll be closing my office door but will be available in two hours" or "I'd love to come but I have too much on my plate—maybe next time."

3. Act accordingly. Follow through. Close the office door. Don't go to the event. Remove yourself from the situation that makes you uncomfortable.

Things to Avoid When Setting Boundaries

1. Assumptions and unspoken expectations. Assuming that people think like you and will behave like you is a recipe for disappointment and resentment. Expressing your needs and expectations is key when setting boundaries. It also sets the ground for a fair interaction, since people can't read your mind or guess your boundaries.

2. Saying one thing but doing the other. If you don't follow through on the boundaries you set, you send the message that your boundaries don't matter—to yourself or to others. It undermines the credibility of all your boundaries, not just the one you're being inconsistent about. So it's important for your words to match your actions. For example, if you warn someone during an argument that you will leave if they continue raising their voice, then you need to leave if they do.

3. Making others responsible for your boundaries. You are in charge of your own boundaries. Others are in charge of theirs. Don't give your power away by expecting others to identify and respect your boundaries for you. Hopefully, they will be thoughtful and considerate. But it's your job to know your boundaries, speak them, and act in accordance with them.

4. Never tolerate abuse. Emotional or physical abuse is never okay, regardless of the state of your own boundaries. Never blame yourself if it happens, and seek help if you find yourself in an abusive relationship.

BOUNDARY CHECK-IN: On a scale of 1 to 10, rate your effectiveness at setting boundaries (1 is you feel completely unable to follow the dos and don'ts above and 10 is you feel you've mastered them).

1	2	3	4	5	6	7	8	9	10

It's also important to keep in mind that, unfortunately, not everyone has the capability or willingness to respect your boundaries once you've set them. They may have unhealthy boundaries themselves, and they may even feel threatened by yours. Whatever the reason, you'll want to limit your interactions with such people. If they are family members or close friends who will stay in your life, you'll need to maintain emotional boundaries of some sort to protect yourself from their unwillingness or inability to engage in a healthier dynamic. For example, you may want to abstain from talking about certain topics or reduce the amount of time you spend with them.

Exploring Your Own Boundaries

1. How can you use self-awareness to increase your ability to set healthy boundaries? This might mean asking more questions while dating or refusing to pursue relationships with people who don't treat you well.

....

....

....

....

2. How can you use shame resilience to increase your ability to set healthy boundaries? This can mean saying no to something you're not okay with, even though feelings of shame arise.

3. How have overly rigid or poor boundaries negatively affected your relationships and your life? For example, have you sacrificed your own well-being for the sake of maintaining harmony in relationships?

4. How might embracing healthier boundaries benefit you? For example, will the way you spend your time become more enjoyable?

THE **VULNERABILITY** WORKBOOK

Healthy vs. Unhealthy Boundaries in Daily Life

People set or fail to set boundaries on a regular basis, whether they're at work or at home and whether they're with platonic friends or in a romantic relationship. Explore the case studies below to get an idea of what boundaries can look like in daily life.

CASE STUDY 1

Ava works for a startup company. The days are sometimes chaotic and fast-paced, but she loves her job and her coworkers. Plus, she never gets bored. But the workload has crept up on her, and her role keeps evolving. She was hired as a marketer, but now she is increasingly involved in the account management and client facets of projects. She also offered to help organize the team holiday party as a side project. She doesn't mind any of it, as it's been good experience to dabble in other areas, and their team is so understaffed that it would be hard to stick to a rigid job description.

She feels that it's starting to be a lot, though. She is staying at the office later and later these days and even dreams about work. She keeps being paranoid that she's going to forget about a deadline or deliverable because she has so much on her plate. And she's been skipping her lunch-break workouts to focus on holiday party planning tasks. To top it off, her coworker Diego, who is responsible for managing social media for the company, just emailed her about involving her in a new campaign. Reading his email, Ava feels a pang of stress. She doesn't have the bandwidth to contribute to this project but feels that she can't say no.

1. In what ways is Ava demonstrating poor boundaries with others?

....

....

....

....

2. In what ways is Ava demonstrating poor boundaries with herself?

3. What are some possible reasons for Ava's poor boundaries?

4. What are Ava's needs, and how are these showing up through her emotions?

THE VULNERABILITY WORKBOOK

5. How could Ava use self-awareness and shame resilience to set healthy boundaries for herself?

6. How could Ava communicate those boundaries at work?

7. What actions could Ava take to uphold healthy boundaries in the workplace?

Jared's new girlfriend, Daphne, has been sleeping over quite a bit of late. At first they were seeing each other a few times a week and had sleepovers on the weekends, a balance that Jared quite appreciated. It allowed him to have alone time during the week and enjoy Daphne's company during the weekend. But now Daphne has been leaving more and more of her things at his apartment, and she has slept over three weeknights in a row. Jared doesn't know what to say without offending her, but he feels increasingly uneasy. It's a feeling of suffocation, as if his individuality is being threatened. In fact, he is starting to feel annoyed by Daphne's presence and is questioning the entire relationship. He breaks up with her.

1. In what ways does Jared have weak boundaries?

....

....

....

....

....

2. In what ways are his boundaries also overly rigid?

....

....

....

....

....

3. What are some possible reasons for Jared's unhealthy boundaries?

_____

_____

_____

_____

4. How did this lack of healthy boundaries negatively affect his relationship with Daphne?

.

_____

_____

_____

_____

5. What were some of Jared's needs in that relationship?

_____

_____

_____

_____

6. How could he have communicated those needs to Daphne and renegotiated the relationship instead of breaking up with her?

....

....

....

....

CASE STUDY 3

Shantelle and Karolina have been best friends since childhood. Karolina has recently gained a new enthusiasm for fitness. She has been very strict about her healthy diet and has lost a bunch of weight. The two friends are catching up over dinner when Shantelle orders dessert. "Do you know how many calories are in that thing?" says Karolina. Shantelle laughs it off. "I don't care, calories don't count when it comes to my favorite cheesecake." Karolina takes a serious tone and says, "Well, your wedding is coming up, and I just want you to feel good in your dress."

Shantelle is shocked that Karolina would comment on her eating choices and body. "I know you've been super into healthy eating and fitness lately and it's awesome, but can you please avoid commenting on my food choices and body? I don't feel comfortable with that." Karolina immediately apologizes and responds that it's true that she's been obsessed with her new habits and that she will be mindful of not making comments like that in the future.

1. How did Shantelle demonstrate healthy boundaries?

....

....

....

....

THE **VULNERABILITY** WORKBOOK

2. How do you think this benefited her relationship with Karolina?

3. What if Shantelle had abstained from expressing her boundary? How could it have negatively impacted her relationship with Karolina in the long run?

4. How did Shantelle's boundary allow for a renegotiation of the interaction and relationship?

Establishing Healthy Boundaries on a Regular Basis

The previous insights may have revealed action steps and habits that you need to embrace to establish healthy boundaries in various areas of your own life or with certain people. Set those boundaries and take note of what happens when you do so.

1. Are there situations that require a renegotiation of boundaries in your life right now? How can you approach such a situation and express yourself?

ACTION STEP 1:

ACTION STEP 2:

ACTION STEP 3:

2. Are there people who continuously disregard your boundaries? How can you make those relationships safer for yourself, knowing these people might not be willing or capable of respecting the boundaries you set?

ACTION STEP 1:

ACTION STEP 2:

ACTION STEP 3:

THE VULNERABILITY WORKBOOK

3. Are there areas of your life where you need to set more boundaries with yourself? What can you do to improve these areas?

ACTION STEP 1:

ACTION STEP 2:

ACTION STEP 3:

Chapter 6
ANCHORING SELF-TRUST

It would be impossible to discuss vulnerability without talking about trust. Chances are, you are at your most vulnerable around people that you trust and feel safe exposing yourself to emotionally. This is healthy—and in this chapter you'll learn why.

In Chapter 5, you reflected on boundaries and the way they support you in feeling safer, thus facilitating the expression of vulnerability. And in the same vein that boundaries provide added safety, so does trust. When someone demonstrates trustworthiness, you can increase your level of vulnerability with them. When someone demonstrates untrustworthiness, you can decrease it. It's like having access to a vulnerability dial that you adjust depending on the emotional safety of the situation—and it never needs to be all-or-nothing.

However, it's common to have a wonky dial. If you're a human being, you've been betrayed or disappointed, sometimes in traumatizing ways. And some of those experiences may have eroded your sense of trust in life and in others. They may even have distorted your sense of trust in yourself. "How did I not see this coming?" or "I should've known better" are examples of thoughts you might have after being betrayed or blindsided, showing how such events can impact your ability to trust yourself to make the right decisions.

It's important to note that painful past experiences can be constructive and make you wiser. But they can also make you consciously or unconsciously internalize black-and-white "always" or "never" beliefs about trust. And such beliefs end up causing more harm than good in the long run. For example, "people always betray me" or "never trust anyone but yourself" are internalized beliefs around the expectation that nobody, under any circumstance, should ever be trusted. If you carry those beliefs, you will experience blockages when trying to be vulnerable with people, even with someone who is actually trustworthy. And you'll prevent meaningful, satisfying moments of connection from happening. Those moments of connection are the tissue that weaves meaningful, satisfying relationships together. So the ability to trust is an essential ingredient of this vulnerability journey.

But what are you supposed to do if your concept of trust has indeed been affected by past emotional pain? And how are you supposed to tell whom you should trust if you've been burned before? Enter self-trust.

Even though you can consciously choose those with whom you want to be vulnerable, at the end of the day you can't control others or predict their every move. A person can have a history of consistent, trustworthy behavior and still end up doing something that breaks your trust. Sometimes there is just no way to see it coming. The point is not to be afraid or close yourself off, but to derive your sense of trust from something more powerful than external circumstances that you can't control.

If you feel solid about your ability to be vulnerable based on the idea that you can either trust people or not, you're setting yourself up for failure if someone does something unpredictable. Which happens—because humans are complex, flawed, and dealing with their own issues. While there is something to be said about discernment—a concept we will dive into in a later chapter—building your ability to be vulnerable around trust in yourself is better than building it around trust in others.

Self-trust is a sense of profound assurance that no matter what happens, you can handle it. That you will bounce back without blaming yourself or closing yourself off to the idea of vulnerability. That you will end up being okay regardless of other people's actions. The more self-trust you have, the safer you will feel about being vulnerable. And in one way or another, the tools you've been picking up on your journey are all helping you develop an unshakable inner foundation that lets you interact with the outside world with greater tolerance for its uncertainty—and therefore greater capacity for vulnerability. Self-trust is yet another tool in your arsenal.

In this chapter, you'll explore what self-trust feels and looks like—and how to anchor a profound sense of trust in yourself and in your ability to navigate life with courage and vulnerability. You will learn what builds self-trust and what erodes it, allowing you to embrace habits that increase your self-trust.

What Is Self-Trust?

Simply put, self-trust is faith in yourself and your abilities.

In her book *The Courage to Trust: A Guide to Building Deep and Lasting Relationships,* psychotherapist Cynthia Wall writes that trusting yourself means "you take care of your own needs and safety and are a loving force in your life."[10] According to Wall, self-trust requires a combination of the following beliefs:

- A belief in your ability to know what you're feeling and thinking—and your ability to express your thoughts and feelings thoughtfully

---

10 Cynthia L. Wall, *The Courage to Trust: A Guide to Building Deep and Lasting Relationships* (Oakland, CA: New Harbinger Publications, 2005).

- A belief in your own integrity—the idea that you follow an ethical code that sustains you even when it's difficult

- A belief in your ability to identify when to take care of yourself and when to take care of others

- A belief in the value of mistakes as teachers—you understand you can't avoid them but you are willing to pick yourself up and try again

- A belief in the value of being open to feedback while also making your own choices

- A belief that you know what you want and that you'll go for it in ways that don't limit others from doing the same

The Benefits of Self-Trust

Self-trust lets you make decisions without second-guessing yourself. It helps you bounce back from hardship and setbacks and allows you to remain hopeful about the future, even when the present moment is bleak. And it makes it easier to relate to others. As relationship experts Linda and Charlie Bloom say in an article in *Psychology Today*, "There is a difference between a life that is grounded in self-trust and one that is not."

According to the Blooms, "When we look at examples of people who are self-trusting, we find that they have clarity and confidence in their choices. They are interdependent, which includes healthy dependency, but not overly dependent or hyper-independent. They speak with authority that comes from a deep place within but is not arrogant. They are good observers and have cultivated the ability to learn from their experiences, both the successes and failures."[11]

Ironically, when you know that you don't need others in order to be happy, functional, and resilient, it's easier to depend on them. When you trust yourself, it's easier to trust others. Being let down may hurt, but you know that it won't have a catastrophic impact on your life because you have your own back, no matter what.

On the other hand, if you are terrified of trusting others, you may not possess the fundamental self-trust that lets you know that if something bad happens, you'll still be okay. Perhaps you don't really believe that. Perhaps you believe that if you do trust others and something bad happens, you won't be able to go on.

---

11 Linda and Charlie Bloom, "Self-Trust and How to Build It," in *Psychology Today*, September 12, 2019. https://www.psychologytoday.com/us/blog/stronger-the-broken-places/201909/self-trust-how-build-it.

Remember shame resilience? Increasing your tolerance for feeling shame breeds greater vulnerability, because it is the fear of vulnerability that is protecting you from potential shame. Knowing that you can feel shame and survive, even if it's unpleasant, tames that fear.

The same can be said about the fear of trusting others and then being let down. By accepting that you'll inevitably be let down at some point and building the belief that you can go through that kind of disappointment and be all right, even if it hurts, you'll feel more relaxed about trusting others. And when you do, you'll feel more relaxed about being vulnerable with them. This is how trusting yourself encourages vulnerability.

REFLECTION

1. What are some "aha" moments as far as your level of self-trust and how it affects your life?

....

....

....

....

2. How does your level of self-trust show up in your inner talk? What are the thoughts you have about yourself on a daily basis?

....

....

....

....

3. What consequences do those thoughts have on your life?

....

....

....

....

4. How would increasing self-trust support you on your vulnerability journey?

....

....

....

....

What Builds Self-Trust and What Erodes It

To sum up, self-trust has different dimensions. It can be understood both as an emotion within the realm of confidence, certainty, and clarity and as a state of mind within the realm of self-awareness (knowing yourself) and self-belief (believing in yourself). Luckily, it's also actionable, so you can develop your own self-trust. Here are habits that build it.

1. Keep your promises to yourself. You trust others when they demonstrate consistency between their words and their actions and follow through on their commitments. The same can be said about your trust toward yourself. To build self-trust, make small promises that you know you can keep. Follow through, and then repeat with bigger commitments. Don't make unrealistic promises to yourself that you won't be able to deliver on.

2. Tune into your own compass for decision-making. If you want to become a self-trusting person, make lots of decisions. Practice tuning into your inner guidance. Connect to your intuition around what is best for you and what you want to do in different situations. If you often struggle with analysis paralysis or tend to feel more comfortable when others are calling the shots, get out of your comfort zone by leading the way and making decisions more quickly. Experience—which sometimes involves messing up—is the only way to learn to rely on your own judgment.

3. Practice self-care. If someone treated you badly, would that make you trust them more or less? Treat yourself well if you want to trust yourself. This includes sleep hygiene, healthy habits like eating nutritious meals and moving your body, financial health, going to doctor appointments when necessary, and tending to your emotional well-being. Take time for yourself on a regular basis. Acknowledge your needs and act on them.

4. Be aware of your self-talk. You can't be self-assured if you constantly talk yourself down. Pay attention to your inner dialogue. Notice when you are unnecessarily harsh with yourself. Aim to speak to yourself as you would talk to a best friend.

***

Keep in mind that the opposite of the habits listed above is also true. If you consistently make promises to yourself but fail to follow through, it will harm your sense of self-trust. If you always look outside of yourself to make decisions and excessively ask others for advice on what to do, you'll erode your ability to trust yourself. If you neglect taking care of yourself, you'll be less self-trusting. And if your self-talk is harsh and you often beat yourself up mentally, you will undermine your capacity for self-trust.

ACTIVITY

1. Think of 5 to 10 ways to help start building more self-trust:

....

....

....

....

....

....

....

....

2. Now choose one habit that could help increase your self-trust and implement it for the rest of the time it takes you to complete this workbook. For example, you may decide to follow through on all your promises to yourself and others. If you say you are going to go to the gym, go to the gym. If you have an appointment, honor your commitment. Alignment between words and actions works wonders for boosting self-trust. Or you might choose to embrace the habit of relying on yourself instead of external input for decision-making, even for something as small as choosing a restaurant to go to. Connecting to your inner compass for making decisions will make you more self-trusting in a variety of situations.

THE **VULNERABILITY** WORKBOOK

3. Improving your self-care or self-talk is helpful for increasing self-trust. Choose one habit that has to do with self-care (such as sleeping eight hours a night) or one habit that has to do with self-talk (noticing each time you are unkind to yourself in your mind and reframing the dialogue to something more positive), and implement that positive change for the rest of the time it takes you to complete this workbook.

HABIT 1: ....

....

HABIT 2: ....

....

Self-Trust and Vulnerability in Action

If you're still wrapping your head around the idea of trusting yourself and what it means on your vulnerability journey, take a look at the case studies below, which highlight what can happen when you trust yourself in life, as well as the possible impact of shaky self-trust.

CASE STUDY 1

Afua has been single for two years after a devastating breakup. Her ex-fiancé cheated on her and left her. She was blindsided and spent months healing and putting the pieces of her life back together. She feels ready to start dating again, and she's been on several first dates with different men. It's been great to break the ice and put herself out there, but she hasn't liked any of them enough to go on a second date. Until now. She just met a man named William, and they had an amazing date and natural chemistry. The conversation flowed organically, and he seems to have many of the qualities she would like in a potential partner.

William just texted to tell her he'd had a great time and would love to see her again. She is about to reply and make plans with him when she has a feeling of dread in the pit of her stomach. Her throat tightens, and she hesitates and then puts her phone down. What if Will seems like a nice guy but turns out to be a liar and a cheater, like her ex? Is it even worth going on a second date? And how would she even know? She thought her ex was a good guy, too. Afua texts her best friend, Brielle, for advice. What should she do next? Should she wait a couple of days to text him back?

1. How does Afua's lack of self-trust reveal itself when she is about to text William?

2. Why do you think her lack of self-trust showed up at that moment?

3. How is her lack of self-trust affecting her behavior with William?

4. How could that have a negative impact on her potential relationship with him?

....

....

....

....

5. What about her relationships in general?

....

....

....

....

6. How could increasing her self-trust help Afua navigate dating?

....

....

....

....

7. What would someone who is self-trusting tell themself in Afua's shoes?

_____

_____

_____

_____

_____

8. What would someone self-trusting do next?

_____

_____

_____

_____

_____

CASE STUDY 2

Ravi has expressed interest in a promotion at work. His boss, Angela, just emailed to offer him a new project. The assignment is outside of Ravi's usual role and comfort zone, and the implication is that the project would give him the opportunity to prove himself with bigger responsibilities. As the project's lead, Ravi would have to devise a strategic plan to increase the customer base of a new product. Ravi is both thrilled and nervous. He has two weeks to put together a presentation for Angela and pitch his strategy.

His colleague Kevin keeps giving him ideas to help him out, and while Ravi is receptive to Kevin's suggestions, his instinct is telling him to take a very specific direction. He looks at available data to validate his intuition, and it only helps him feel more confident about his plan. Granted, he's never tested this plan before and it's a little scary, since he would be the one responsible for its success or potential failure. However, he also reminds himself that he has 10 years of experience in his field, and that his background as a web developer gives him an advantageous perspective at work. He thanks Kevin for his feedback, uses some of it to strengthen his plan, and finalizes his presentation.

1. How is Ravi's self-trust revealing itself in a situation that is out of his comfort zone?

2. What are some key indicators of Ravi's self-trust in the way he is dealing with this project?

3. How is his self-trust helping him navigate this exciting yet scary career opportunity?

4. In what ways will self-trust help him execute his plan and ensure the success of his strategy?

5. What might someone less self-trusting have done in Ravi's shoes?

6. How could a lack of self-trust negatively impact a career opportunity such as this?

Stephanie is very proud of her independence. In fact, she often boasts about the fact that she doesn't need anyone—especially not a romantic partner. She is single and free and likes it that way. She has casual flings here and there, but every time someone starts to develop feelings for her and things get a little more serious, she shuts down and ends the relationship. This usually happens when the person she is dating starts to express feelings and needs and ask about hers. She doesn't like talking about her feelings, and she doesn't want to feel responsible for the emotional state of others, either.

Stephanie had one serious relationship a few years back. She was hopelessly in love and thought she would spend the rest of her life with her ex. Remembering how needy and desperate she felt makes her shudder. She would call her ex nonstop, be paranoid about her whereabouts and jealous of her speaking to other women, and just feel like a total mess. She has no interest in being in that position again.

1. How is Stephanie's lack of self-trust revealing itself in her love life, both in her past relationship and in her present casual flings?

2. How is Stephanie's extreme independence actually a shield for her low self-trust?

3. Why do you think she keeps romantic interests at arm's length?

4. How would someone self-trusting handle a conversation with a romantic interest who wants to discuss feelings and needs?

5. How could increasing her self-trust help Stephanie navigate her love life—and the vulnerable conversations that she now finds uncomfortable?

6. How could increasing her self-trust benefit her life in the long run?

Assessing Your Self-Trust

Now that you've wrapped your head around the idea of self-trust and the way it can affect you on your vulnerability journey, it's time to assess just how self-trusting you are and where there are areas for improvement.

1. In which areas of your life do you feel the most self-trusting? Why?

2. In which areas of your life do you lack self-trust? Why?

3. Reflect on a time when your lack of self-trust negatively affected your ability to be vulnerable. What happened? How did you feel? What did you do? How did it impact the situation?

....

....

....

....

4. Think of a time when being self-trusting helped you to be more vulnerable. What happened? How did you feel? What did you do? How did it impact the situation?

....

....

....

....

Boosting Your Self-Trust

Wherever you are on the scale of self-trust, keeping up with your new habits is going to be key. Now you will choose one more practice to implement as you move forward, using your self-trust strengths to improve areas in which your self-trust is weak.

ACTIVITY

1. Based on your answers to the previous questions, take note of the areas of your life where self-trust comes easier than it does in others. Transfer one practice from an area where it comes easy to a more challenging area. As an example, if you noticed that you trust yourself at work because you are super decisive and have confidence in your own judgment, you may want to consider being more decisive and trusting your judgment in your dating life.

Which habit will you implement, and why?

....

....

....

....

....

....

2. What are some practical ways you can implement this habit in your everyday life?

....

....

....

....

....

....

....

3. Track your progress for three weeks, recording each time you put the new habit into action:

	WEEK 1	WEEK 2	WEEK 3
MONDAY			
TUESDAY			
WEDNESDAY			
THURSDAY			
FRIDAY			
SATURDAY			
SUNDAY			

THE VULNERABILITY WORKBOOK

Chapter 7
MANAGING INTENSE EMOTIONS

You have reached the point in your vulnerability journey where it's relevant to talk about emotions that may be intense or unpleasant. All the tools you've picked up so far have prepared you for this moment. Behind a fear of vulnerability lies a fear of feeling and exposing certain emotions, but the safer you feel through mechanisms such as boundaries and self-trust—which you unpacked in Chapter 5 and Chapter 6—the better equipped you are to experience and express the full range of your emotions.

However, experiencing and expressing the full range of your emotions doesn't mean slamming doors when you feel angry or running away in the middle of a conversation because you feel afraid. Emotional intelligence (also known as EQ) is key for having vulnerable interactions, and the good news is that if you've been diligent about completing the exercises in this workbook, you're well on your way to developing more of it. In case you're wondering, EQ is the ability to perceive, understand, and manage your own emotions while also being aware of the emotions of others. From self-awareness to shame resilience and authentic communication, you've definitely been improving your emotional intelligence through the work you've done so far.

Whether you consider yourself high on the emotional intelligence scale or feel a bit lost when it comes to dealing with emotions, you'll find value in learning to manage your emotions better—especially in moments of high vulnerability when they come out in full swing. Emotions are core to the human experience, yet there is no rulebook for navigating them. Your first teacher was your childhood. If you grew up witnessing your parents having explosive fights, you may be scared of conflict and negative emotions. If you were told to stop crying and toughen up, you may have learned to repress your feelings. Those early experiences shape your emotional responses later in life. Be aware of this, and be gentle with yourself if you identify any unhelpful patterns preventing you from embracing vulnerability.

If other chapters in this workbook had you combatting metaphorical beasts on your vulnerability journey, in this one you'll be befriending them. Emotions are your friend—not your enemy. If you get to know them, you'll see that they contain rich insights that can help you create meaningful moments of connection with yourself and others. Perhaps you've had bad experiences in emotional situations. Those experiences probably turned out that way not because of the emotions themselves but because of your reactions or the reactions of others to them. (More on that in a bit!)

In this chapter you'll learn about the complex world of human emotions. What causes them, and how does this impact your efforts to be vulnerable? What happens when you and another person bring your own subjective emotional experiences into an interaction? And how can you use this information to your advantage? You'll end up feeling better equipped to deal with emotionally charged moments—and thus better equipped to be vulnerable. Keep your pen close by, and let's dive in.

What Causes Emotions?

Joy. Sadness. Anger. Sorrow. Contentment. Frustration. There are so many possible emotions. What causes them, though? Here is a straightforward breakdown of an emotion taking form. Something happens—say a dog lunges toward you. In response, you feel physiological arousal. Perhaps you are startled and afraid, and your heart feels like it's going to jump out of your chest. Then you have a thought: Uh oh, this isn't good. Finally you act, stepping back to avoid the dog.

In the real world, it's a little more complex than that. Yes, there is an event-response cycle that involves arousal processes in your body, cognitive processes in your mind, and behaviors that follow. But the initial stimulus can look very different from a dog attack—not to mention that there are stimuli everywhere.

As an example, you could feel an emotion in response to something someone says. Let's say your sister is complaining about the weight she's gained, and you've been feeling uncomfortable with your own weight. You feel a pang of stress after hearing her say that, and maybe guilt because you've been putting off going to the gym. So you're having those thoughts and feelings in reaction to this random thing your sister said. But meanwhile your cousin, who is also part of the conversation and is perfectly content with her own weight, might not have any noteworthy emotional response to the comment—illustrating why emotions are subjective.

Everyone's experience of life is filtered through the lens of their own subjective emotional experience, which affects what they do and say. But the way you *perceive* what they do and say is filtered through your own emotional experience. No wonder interpersonal scenarios can feel like minefields filled with potential misunderstandings.

Why Understanding Emotions Matters

Understanding how emotional processes take place is critical to being able to manage your own emotions. You can't control something if you're not aware that it's happening. If you can pause and pinpoint when you are having a strong feeling in response to an event, you'll be more likely to be able to regulate your response and be intentional about doing so. This is important when it comes to vulnerability, because when you do or say something that feels vulnerable for you, you'll likely feel all sorts of things. It's part of the territory. But being aware of the feelings you are experiencing and why you are experiencing them will help you choose the best course of action, proactively instead of reactively.

Being in tune with emotions also allows you to be more aware of others and positively influence interpersonal dynamics. Let's go back to the example above. You may realize that your sister is stressed about her own weight and not trying to make you feel bad about yours. You may choose to be vulnerable and say something like, "If I am being honest, I feel really bad hearing you say this because I'm not happy about my weight these days, either. Would it be okay if we focused on being positive about our bodies?" Someone less emotionally intelligent could get mad at the sister for steering the conversation in that direction, because they want to avoid their own discomfort with the topic.

Remember how emotional intelligence is about perceiving, understanding, and managing emotions? Knowing about emotions is, of course, part of that. But having a broad emotional vocabulary is also super important. Being able to label what you are perceiving and to express it when relevant requires a rich emotional vocabulary. Otherwise you may get stuck feeling physiological arousal without being able to pinpoint what you are feeling—which can be quite overwhelming—and end up having your feelings externalized in unhelpful ways. Think of a toddler throwing a tantrum. That's what can happen to you when you are not well-versed in what's going on in your world emotionally and don't have the tools to process it—which starts with being able to label it.

ACTIVITY: MOOD TRACKING

This exercise will help you develop awareness of your emotions and practice labeling them. For the next two days, use this space to check in three times a day to record your mood: once in the morning, once midday, and once in the evening. Also take note of any unexpected emotionally charged moments during the day. What did you feel? How did the emotion show up in your body? How did you react?

	WHAT EMOTION AM I FEELING?	WHERE DO I FEEL IT IN MY BODY?	WHAT HAPPENED?	HOW DID I REACT?
MORNING				
MIDDAY				
EVENING				

THE VULNERABILITY WORKBOOK

	WHAT EMOTION AM I FEELING?	WHERE DO I FEEL IT IN MY BODY?	WHAT HAPPENED?	HOW DID I REACT?
MORNING				
MIDDAY				
EVENING				

What Are Triggers?

You've probably heard of the idea of "being triggered." Sometimes news footage comes with trigger warnings because it contains graphic images that may be upsetting. But what exactly are triggers?

According to the GoodTherapy blog, a trigger is a reminder of past trauma. "This reminder can cause a person to feel overwhelming sadness, anxiety, or panic. It may also cause someone to have flashbacks. A flashback is a vivid, often negative memory that may appear without warning. It can cause someone to lose track of their surroundings and 'relive' a traumatic event."[12]

---

12 "Trigger," GoodTherapy blog, updated May 2, 2018. https://www.goodtherapy.org/blog/psychpedia/trigger.

In mental health terms, triggers are about trauma—such as veterans suffering from post-traumatic stress disorder (PTSD) who get flashbacks of war experiences every time they hear a loud noise. But you don't need to be suffering from PTSD to have emotional triggers. Most people experience them in some shape or form. In this workbook, we use the term to describe any time some past experience taints the present moment with a strong emotional reaction. That's right: some of your most emotionally charged moments aren't about what's happening in front of you but about what happened before and left a strong imprint on you. In fact, if your emotional response to a situation feels disproportionate to what is happening in the present, it may be an indicator that your past is living in your present.

Keep in mind that if you do have unresolved trauma or think that you may be suffering from a condition such as PTSD, it's important to seek professional help to assist you in coping with your symptoms.

Triggers are relevant because they affect your emotional experience, which affects the way you interact with others. Let's bring back the example of the sisters discussing their weight gain. Now let's imagine for a moment that the cousin wasn't completely indifferent to the comment but had an eating disorder as a teenager. In this scenario, the cousin is emotionally triggered by the seemingly harmless weight gain comment.

REFLECTION

1. Think of three situations where you felt particularly emotionally triggered. What happened? Who was there? How did you feel? Why? How did you react?

2. Do these situations have anything in common? What do they tell you about your own triggers? Knowing this, how would you approach similar situations in the future?

....

....

....

....

....

What Are Projections?

Triggers are not the only factors that can influence how an interaction between people unfolds. Enter projections. According to an article in *Psychology Today*, a projection is "the process of displacing one's feelings onto a different person, animal, or object."[13] The term is commonly used to describe "defensive projection," which is when someone attributes traits they dislike about themselves onto others. For example, a cheater may accuse his or her partner of cheating, or a bully may ridicule a target for being sensitive because of an internal struggle with their own sensitivity.

In this workbook, we will be using the term "projection" to describe anytime someone transposes an inner struggle onto an external situation. Again, some of your most emotionally charged moments are not about what is happening in front of you but about an inner conflict that you are transposing onto what is happening.

To illustrate, let's keep building on the example of the cousin who suffered from an eating disorder in her teenage years. She could project her experience onto the sister complaining about her weight and accuse her of having an eating disorder. But someone can complain about weight gain without suffering from an eating disorder. Just because the cousin had one, that doesn't automatically mean that the sister does. Rather, the cousin is projecting her experience onto the sister.

If there is one thing to remember from unpacking such concepts as triggers and projections, it's that there are events and then there are the emotions that we have about those events—which can be

---

13 "Projection," in *Psychology Today*, Sussex Publishers, accessed March 20, 2022. https://www.psychologytoday.com/basics/projection.

triggered or projecting. When emotions are running high, it's sometimes helpful to take a step back and aim to separate the event itself from the meaning you've given to that event. In the example above, the actual event was the sister complaining about her weight. But all the examples that followed showed how different people could have different thoughts about what had been said. And those thoughts influence the emotions that come up and the actions that stem from them.

REFLECTION

1. Think of three situations in which you projected your own inner struggle onto an external situation involving someone else. What happened? Who was there? How did you feel? Why? How did you react?

2. Do these situations have anything in common? What do they tell you about your projection tendencies? Knowing this, how would you approach similar situations in the future?

....

....

....

....

....

Self-Regulation

If you possess the skill of self-regulation, you get to have more control over your emotional state—and that can be very useful when exploring vulnerability. What is self-regulation? A blog post from YourTherapySource describes it as "the ability to monitor and manage your energy states, emotions, thoughts, and behaviors in ways that are acceptable and produce positive results such as well-being, loving relationships, and learning."[14]

Self-regulation requires both self-awareness and emotional intelligence, as well as a certain level of stress tolerance and focus. Arlin Cuncic wrote in a Verywell Mind blog post that "emotional self-regulation refers to the ability to manage disruptive emotions and impulses." According to her, "Self-regulation involves taking a pause between a feeling and an action—taking the time to think things through, make a plan, wait patiently."[15]

Effective strategies for better self-regulating as an adult include mindfulness practices, such as meditating on a regular basis or taking deep breaths and focusing on being present in your body before you react to an emotionally charged situation. Monitor how you are feeling and how you want to react—observe before reacting.

---

14 Leah Kalish, "What Is Self-Regulation?" YourTherapySource, January 19, 2020. https://www
.yourtherapysource.com/blog1/2020/01/19/what-is-self-regulation-2.
15 Arlin Cuncic, "How to Develop and Use Self-Regulation in Your Life." Verywell Mind, updated January 27, 2022.
https://www.verywellmind.com/how-you-can-practice-self-regulation-4163536.

It's also useful to reframe your thoughts about the situation. Are the thoughts you are having causing added emotional distress? Are they the actual truth, or could there be an alternative explanation?

Remember the intentions you set for this vulnerability journey in Chapter 1. How can you act in a way that is aligned with your ultimate vulnerability vision despite any uncomfortable emotions you may be experiencing in the present moment?

While it can be challenging at times, and you don't have control over everything in your environment or what other people do, you do have some control over your own actions. Self-regulation allows you to stay intentional and not let intense emotions get the best of you.

ACTIVITY: MINDFULNESS PRACTICE

Make a list of activities that make you feel present, grounded, and calm. Perhaps drawing or coloring does that for you. Maybe you enjoy yoga. Choose one activity and add it to your daily or weekly routine for improved self-regulation.

Triggers, Projections, and Self-Regulation in Action

Study the situations below to gain a deeper understanding of the way triggers, projections, and self-regulation can be intertwined in different situations—and how they affect someone's ability to be vulnerable.

CASE STUDY 1

Andy and Desiree are getting ready to go to a fundraiser hosted by Andy's workplace. Desiree is putting the finishing touches on her outfit. But she has forgotten that the party has an all-white theme. Andy walks into the bedroom, notices Desiree in a red dress, and says, "You're not wearing that, are you?" Desiree feels an intense, unpleasant feeling—her cheeks flush and her pulse accelerates. Her whole body is tensing up, and she wants to snap at Andy. How dare he tell her what to wear?

But Desiree quickly realizes what her reaction is all about. The man she dated before Andy was very controlling, and he would feel threatened whenever she dressed up or wore a bold color such as red. That would usually lead to fights, because he would ask her to change. It's not like Andy to comment on her clothing—in fact, he always tells her that she looks great in anything she chooses to wear. Understanding that she is feeling triggered, she takes a deep breath and asks Andy: "Yes, I was planning on wearing this. Why? What's wrong with it?" Andy then reminds her of the all-white theme.

1. Separate the event (what happened) from Desiree's interpretation of it (what she thought and how she felt about what happened).

2. What was Desiree's trigger?

3. How did Desiree use self-regulation?

4. What could have happened had Desiree been less self-aware and more reactive?

5. How could Desiree use this moment as an opportunity to embrace vulnerability and connect with Andy on a deeper level?

Luisa was raised in a conservative environment. She was brought up with the notion that sex is shameful, and that women should never sleep around if they want to be respected. Luisa is out with girlfriends when the conversation turns a bit raunchy. Sam, who is single and highly comfortable with her own sexuality, is talking about her latest one-night stand. Luisa feels increasingly uneasy. She doesn't know Sam that well, but she is appalled and feels embarrassed on her behalf. Poor Sam isn't classy at all. And what is that outfit? So much cleavage. Does she expect any man to take her seriously? She snaps out of her judgmental train of thought when Sam turns to her, smiles, and says: "Oh, Luisa, I hope I am not offending you. I tend to be super open like that, but I don't mean to be rude or make you uncomfortable." Luisa smiles tightly and tells her it's fine.

1. Separate the event (what happened) from Luisa's interpretation of it (what she thought and how she felt about what happened).

....

....

2. In which ways is Luisa projecting?

....

....

3. How could Luisa use this moment as an opportunity to embrace vulnerability and practice authentic communication with the group of friends?

....

....

Merrick has built a reputation for being the best in his field. He is a commercial interior designer and has landed some of the most prestigious contracts in the country. But he also has a temper. Everyone knows that about him, but they accept his outbursts at work because of his track record for delivering outstanding results. Merrick is working on the design of an upcoming restaurant and is visiting the location for the first time. He parks his car and texts the restaurant manager, who is supposed to be greeting him. Half an hour goes by, and he still hasn't heard from the manager. He is furious and starting to fantasize about getting the manager fired. He's not getting paid to sit around in a parking lot. There is nothing he hates more than waiting—it's a complete lack of respect and disregard of his time. Finally his phone rings. It's the restaurant manager, who explains that he'd had a family emergency and profusely apologizes for the delay. Merrick can't hear him. He can't hear him because he's screaming and threatening to get the manager fired.

1. Separate the event (what happened) from Merrick's interpretation of the event (what he thought and felt about what happened).

....

....

2. How does Merrick's emotional state drive his actions at work?

....

....

3. How could Merrick use self-regulation to have better reactions in the workplace and in life?

....

....

Takeaways on Triggers, Projections, and Self-Regulation

Human emotions can be complex. And managing intense emotions is something you can only truly practice in real time when situations and emotions come up. As you move forward on your vulnerability journey, reflect on some key takeaways that can help you deal with emotionally charged situations in the future.

1. What are some "aha" moments for you as far as triggers, projections, and self-regulation?

....

....

2. What are some key takeaways that can help you manage intense emotions on your vulnerability journey?

....

....

3. Moving forward, what are some strategies that you could implement to navigate emotionally charged moments while embracing vulnerability?

....

....

Chapter 8

USING YOUR DISCERNMENT

Learning about the impact your emotions have on the way you perceive and process reality is a game-changer. While all your emotions are valid, they don't all paint an accurate picture of reality, especially when triggers and projections are involved. But since we are all subjective beings who have subjective experiences of the world, is there such a thing as an ultimate truth? Some things, like gravity, are unquestionable facts. Other things, like interpersonal interactions filtered through the lenses of the different parties involved, are more nuanced. The truth lies somewhere in the middle of multiple coexisting truths.

If you're wondering what these philosophical questions have to do with your vulnerability journey, keep in mind that you are discovering one tool at a time as you work your way through this workbook. The combination of all these tools will help you embrace vulnerability in constructive ways, at appropriate moments, and in different situations. Using your discernment to know how and when to lean into vulnerability is a big piece of the puzzle.

Oxford defines discernment as "the ability to judge well." As you judge when and with whom to be vulnerable, what to say, what to do, what you are feeling, and why you are feeling it, you'll want to avoid falling into the trap of confusing emotions for reality. Sometimes, though, your emotions actually will be right, giving you clues as to what to do.

Discernment is about being able to tell the difference. When are you projecting and when is someone actually behaving in ways that are problematic? When are you overreacting because you're being triggered, and when are your reactions justified because someone has violated one of your boundaries? It all depends on the context.

To discern is thus to solidify your self-trust. It's a tool that will let you embody a lot of the other tools on your vulnerability tool belt and bring them into real-life situations in actionable ways. For

THE **VULNERABILITY** WORKBOOK

example, you might find yourself in the middle of a conversation where you recognize with certainty that being vulnerable would benefit you and the other people involved. Though it might feel scary and uncomfortable to share something that makes you vulnerable, you recognize that by not doing so you'd be avoiding the threat of potential shame, and you decide to lean into your shame resilience and proceed. You trust yourself to be okay no matter what happens. You say the vulnerable thing, and others respond. You assess their responses and lean into everything you've learned so far to navigate the next steps. That level of certainty, that awareness of yourself and others, and that ability to know how to act and react can only be facilitated with the aid of a healthy dose of discernment.

In this chapter you'll learn how to use your discernment to be vulnerable—or not. Even if you feel unsure because this whole vulnerability thing is new to you, you'll find out how to rely on certain benchmarks to strengthen your ability to be a discerning person. And you'll unpack how discernment, authentic communication, boundaries, and self-trust can come out to play on this vulnerability journey and benefit your relationships.

Ready? Congratulate yourself for getting so far into this process, and then dive in.

What Is Discernment?

Discernment is ultimately about decision-making. It's being able to recognize the differences between objects, people, and situations, with all their intricacies, and then using your judgment to interact with them accordingly. "To me, discernment is the ability to notice objective differences among stimuli (activities, people, objects, etc.) along relevant dimensions," wrote Raj Raghunathan in *Psychology Today*.[16]

According to Raghunathan, professor of marketing at the University of Texas in Austin, the quality of our decisions depends on the quality of our discernments. And discerning differences among human beings is more important than anything else we might discern, since decisions involving humans have the greatest impact on our well-being.

Embracing vulnerability can be challenging if you've been burned in the past. Maybe you unknowingly chose to be vulnerable with unsafe people—people who took advantage of your vulnerability. Perhaps you have felt the sting of being shamed for being vulnerable and the pain of being rejected or ridiculed for it. Being discerning won't guarantee that you'll never get burned again. But it *will* help you make decisions that support you and improve your relationships. It means that you walk on this vulnerability journey with wisdom. That your perceptiveness allows you to judge things accurately before you make

---

16 Raj Raghunathan, "Don't Be Judgmental, Be Discerning," *Psychology Today*, May 10, 2011. https://www .psychologytoday.com/ca/blog/sapient-nature/201105/dont-be-judgmental-be-discerning.

a decision about an interaction or a relationship, sifting through emotions, words, and behaviors and then carrying yourself forward accordingly.

REFLECTION

1. Do you consider yourself to be a discerning person when it comes to people? Why or why not?

　　　　THE **VULNERABILITY** WORKBOOK

2. Think of three situations in which your discernment has served you well when relating with others. For example, maybe you realized that you had misjudged a coworker and changed your approach with that person. What happened? How did it serve you and your relationships?

3. Think of three situations in which you didn't use your discernment when relating with others. For example, maybe you ignored red flags while dating someone. What happened? How did it harm you and your relationships?

....

....

....

....

....

....

....

....

....

When Discernment Meets Other Vulnerability Pillars

As mentioned above, your discernment is particularly useful in combination with some of the other vulnerability pillars you've been learning about. For one thing, it's an important way to strengthen self-trust. The more you trust your ability to judge well, the more you trust yourself to navigate emotionally charged, vulnerable situations with others. Moments of vulnerability that used to be unnerving will become less of a big deal to you. And while moments of profound vulnerability may still feel scary, you will feel more equipped to deal with them.

Boundaries also come into play when using your discernment, because you will be able to know when to harden a boundary or when to soften one. And as for authentic communication, being a discerning person will support you on that front, too. You will feel more confident in your ability to express yourself authentically, because you'll trust your judgment about what you are communicating and why, regardless of how others may react.

In other words, discernment is almost like a superpower for navigating the complex world of human relationships. But it's not as if being discerning is as simple as snapping your fingers. If anything, it's almost easier *not* to be discerning when you consider how triggers and projections can influence your interactions with others. What if you think you're being discerning but in fact you're being triggered? What if you think you're judging well but are projecting instead? Emotions can muddy the waters and make it that much more complex to use discernment to make constructive decisions.

Don't be discouraged, though. There are things you can do to become all the wiser. Discernment comes from both intuition and experience, and you already possess those two things if you are working your way through this workbook. It's just about awakening them.

How to Become More Discerning

Let's start by talking about intuition. It's possible that you've been conditioned to believe that relying on your intuition—that inner voice or inner knowing that guides you without needing any form of validation—is an inferior form of decision-making. That you should be making decisions using only logic. But there is value in instincts. It's just that when you've spent a lifetime purposefully drowning out your instincts, quieting down that inner voice that just "knows," you're no longer able to discern when your intuition is giving you valid clues.

At least once in your life, you've probably experienced a moment when you felt that something was just "off" with another person. Maybe you brushed that feeling away and ignored it because you had no concrete reason to believe it, and nothing to back it up. And then you discovered that there was indeed cause for concern. Intuition can protect you. It can help you discern. Don't think of it as a fluffy concept but rather as a sharpened form of intelligence that is always getting smarter by absorbing cues, without your even being aware of that process going on in the background. The more you get to know how your intuition shows up and how it looks, sounds, and feels, the more you can rely on it to be discerning.

REFLECTION

1. How connected to your intuition are you? Do you feel comfortable relying on it for decisions?

2. Think of three times when you followed your intuition to make a decision, big or small, in any area of your life. Maybe you trusted your gut about a career change. Or followed your intuition about whether to open up to someone. What happened? How did following your intuition turn out?

3. Think of three times when you did not follow your intuition to make a decision, big or small, in any area of your life. Perhaps you accepted a job even though you had a gut feeling it was the wrong fit. Maybe you knew you didn't want to go to a party but went anyway. What happened? How did not following your intuition turn out?

4. How does your intuition show up for you? For example, you may feel a gut instinct about just what to do. You may have a sudden insight.

5. How does your intuition feel in your body? Perhaps you feel a sense of calm certitude, for example.

6. What are some telltale signs that you are not tapping into your intuition? Do you overanalyze situations and feel paralyzed about making a decision? Or do you ask everyone for advice on what you should do?

How Experience Informs Discernment

Now let's turn to the second aspect of discernment: experience. Experience makes you wiser. It's a great way to validate what your intuition is telling you, too. For example, if someone has taken advantage of your vulnerability in the past, perhaps to get something from you, you may have looked back on that situation and learned from it. You may have identified red flags that you hadn't seen before that.

The tricky thing here (as you may recall from the self-trust chapter) is to avoid letting past wounds turn you into an overly paranoid person who always assumes the worst. That would be distorted, not discerning. When you are discerning, you don't want to put on rose-colored glasses but you also don't want to catastrophize. Experience can give you the wisdom to make contextual judgment calls.

REFLECTION

1. What memorable experiences have you had in terms of being vulnerable with other people? What are the top three that come to mind? Perhaps you once declared your love to a friend. Or maybe you decided to be very honest with a family member with whom you have a complicated relationship.

2. How did those experiences shape your discernment when it comes to vulnerability? Maybe you learned not to idealize romantic partners. Or you realized that a particular friendship was toxic for you, and that made you more intentional about the friends you choose.

3. Do you tend either to put on rose-colored glasses or to catastrophize? How and why? If not, what makes you confident in your own judgment?

_____

_____

_____

_____

_____

***

There is no straightforward step-by-step process to becoming more discerning. But learning to recognize the voice of your intuition and to derive wisdom from your own life experiences are two essential aspects of using your discernment. And everything else you've been reflecting on and practicing on your path through this workbook will also help strengthen your ability to discern when it comes to people and vulnerability.

What Discernment Can Look Like in Relationships

Using your discernment in the context of relationships is a subtle yet crucial practice. The case studies below demonstrate the way being discerning can support different decisions within interactions with others.

CASE STUDY 1

Margot has been going to therapy for a few years to learn how to relate to others in more secure ways. She has a history of being attracted to people who mirror the dysfunction she experienced in her childhood home: men who invalidate her emotional needs and manipulate her. Her mother was very much like that, providing conditional love and using emotions to control her children. Because of her past, Margot struggles when it comes to intimacy and vulnerability. She is afraid of being attracted to the wrong men, and it's hard for her to open up without feeling that intimacy is a threat to her well-being. She now feels ready to be in a healthy romantic relationship, and with the support of her therapist she is navigating the world of dating in a more conscious way. She has been getting to know two different men and taking things slowly. With Greyson, she feels this intoxicating chemistry, but it's also unnerving. She constantly worries about what to do next or what he could possibly think. With Robert, she feels relaxed and safe but doesn't experience intense butterflies.

Margot wonders if her attraction to Greyson is unhealthy—her gut kind of tells her it is. She has been practicing authentic communication and boundaries with him, and in one conversation about defining the expectations of their relationship, she notices that something is off. He avoids directly answering her questions and offers vague non-answers to skirt the topic.

Margot realizes that based on her history, she should be careful about not letting her intense chemistry with Greyson cloud her judgment. She has just met him, after all, and doesn't know him that well. She reflects on their interactions and concludes that his behavior in conversations is concerning and doesn't support the type of relationship she wants to create, one in which she feels heard, seen, and valued. Margot decides that the healthiest thing for her is to end things with him and focus on exploring her relationship with Robert, with whom she feels much safer.

1. How is Margot actively using her discernment while navigating her romantic connections?

....

....

....

....

2. How is Margot using both intuition and experience to make decisions?

....

....

....

....

3. What are some of Margot's challenges when it comes to discerning?

4. What could have happened with Greyson if Margot had been less discerning?

5. Do you think Margot made the right call? Why or why not?

CASE STUDY 2

James and Onkar are coworkers. They are in different departments and have been tasked with collaborating on a project. They get along well and are starting to get to know each other on a more personal level. They have meetings all the time and need to talk about the project daily, after all. James feels inclined to let the friendship that's building organically with Onkar develop. But what Onkar doesn't know is that James went through a terrible time in his last job. He was burned out and had to quit after experiencing workplace bullying. The worst of it was that a coworker he thought was a friend ended up falsely accusing James of being a bully. James had confided in this friend, so the betrayal stung. He is now afraid to open up to people at work.

One afternoon, Onkar asks James if he wants to grab drinks after work. He notices James' hesitation and says, "Hey, no pressure! I just thought it might be fun to check out that new bar around the corner and decompress before going home. I totally get it if you don't feel like it." James feels himself close up, but he realizes that he could use a work friend and that Onkar has given him no reason not to trust him. He also remembers that he doesn't have to share more with Onkar until he gets to know him better. It's just drinks, and he's in control of how much information he's comfortable divulging. "No, sounds like a great plan!" he tells Onkar. "See you later."

1. How did Onkar display discernment in this interaction?

_____

_____

_____

_____

2. How did James use discernment in this interaction?

3. How did that benefit James?

4. In what ways did James lean on self-trust and boundaries to overcome his fear of being vulnerable with Onkar?

5. What could James have missed out on by completely shutting down and declining the invite?

....

....

....

....

CASE STUDY 3

Florence considers herself to be an open-minded, highly empathetic person. When she meets Tobias on a dating app and feels instantly intrigued by his music career and his lifestyle, which involves traveling around with his band, she is excited to see where things could go. They meet in person and start dating. She loves Tobias' passion for music and can listen to him speak about it for hours. She doesn't notice that Tobias never seems to ask any questions about her. When he starts messaging her daily, she is flattered by the attention. So she is hurt when he all of a sudden pulls back and disappears for a couple of days, but she tells herself he must have a good reason and that he'll text her back. He does, but he never explains the sudden switch.

Florence is sensing that Tobias has some demon; his mood abruptly changes at times. But she understands that he's probably been through a lot. It sounds like he didn't have the best childhood, from what she has gathered. She doesn't want to pressure him into revealing too much. She tells herself that he'll open up more over time. And they get along so well and have so much fun together. She is falling in love. Then one evening Florence receives an anonymous phone call from a woman claiming to be Tobias' girlfriend. She is completely devastated.

1. How did Florence lack discernment from the beginning of her relationship with Tobias?

_____

_____

_____

_____

_____

2. How did Florence ignore her intuition?

_____

_____

_____

_____

3. How could Florence have used her discernment during her evolving relationship with Tobias?

_____

_____

_____

_____

_____

4. How would that have benefited her?

....

....

....

....

5. How did lacking discernment hurt her?

....

....

....

....

ACTIVITY: FLEXING YOUR DISCERNMENT MUSCLES

For the next two weeks, commit to intentionally using your discernment to make decisions in different relationships and interactions. Take note below of your experiences, insights, and learnings.

Chapter 9

HOLDING SPACE FOR OTHERS

Most of this workbook has taken you on a journey of inner discovery, and there's a reason for that. Even while practicing concepts that pertain to your interactions with the unpredictable outside world and the people in it, you've been focusing mostly on deepening your connection with yourself. This is a necessary prerequisite for deepening your connection with others.

The more aware you are of yourself, the more aware you become of those around you. The more in tune you are with your own emotional state, the more you are able to notice and empathize with the emotional state of others. The more authentically you communicate, the more you open the door for others to communicate authentically with you. As you lead the way with courage and vulnerability, courage and vulnerability follow in your interactions. As you live life more open-heartedly, life opens up to you with heartfelt wonders.

Holding space for others is an important part of reaping the benefits of being more vulnerable. You learn to offer vulnerability and you learn to receive it, and you rejoice in the moments of intimacy that ensue—the moments that make this inner work worthwhile.

But you have to be able to hold space for yourself before being able to do all of that safely and wholeheartedly. Skipping this step is a recipe for the kind of unhealthy overexposure or avoidance discussed in Chapter 5, where we looked at the role of boundaries in being able to embrace constructive vulnerability.

To get back to the analogy of the hero's journey that kick-started this whole process, you have now reached a metaphorical culminating point on your journey: the ordeal before the reward. Why is it an ordeal? If you've been denying your own vulnerability, it's hard to accept the vulnerability of others. If you sometimes find yourself uncomfortable with displays of vulnerability, this chapter will be especially relevant for you.

Interestingly, when you find yourself able to welcome the vulnerability of others with openness, curiosity, and validation (factors that make it flourish), you'll realize that it's a signal that *you* are becoming more vulnerable yourself.

In this chapter you'll work on growing your ability to be a safe space for others. You'll learn to understand the cues and behaviors that encourage vulnerability and the ones that shut it down. You'll learn to recognize inner patterns that may unconsciously make you less of a safe space, enabling you to disarm them and create safety for others to be vulnerable with you. (Yes, there is still inner work involved in *receiving* vulnerability!)

Ready to roll up your sleeves and tackle this last challenge? You're now armed with all the right tools to do so. Being able to hold space for others requires as much practice as being able to hold space for yourself. But you've come this far, so keep aiming for progress over perfection as you hone your skills in real life and beyond the pages of this workbook.

Why Being Able to Receive Vulnerability Is Key

You may be wondering why you should even bother improving your ability to be there for others. That's not a selfish question. It's a fair one, especially if you've struggled with relating in vulnerable, healthy ways in the past. You're putting in the work, so why not let other people do their own work, too, and then everyone will live happily and vulnerably ever after, right?

Every relationship and human interaction is a two-way street. In the most consciously vulnerable form of relating, you are responsible for your side of the street, and the other person is responsible for theirs. That means being self-aware, expressing your needs and communicating authentically, using your discernment, setting boundaries, and so on—everything you've been developing so far, basically.

When all parties involved are intentional about their side of the street, the relationship dynamic benefits from it. You gain a deeper understanding of each other and feel more recognized for who you truly are. Instead of fighting to put up armor and protect yourself from shame, you become part of the same team. The relationship can evolve into a sacred space for authentic self-expression—which feels incredible for everyone involved.

In that sense, you are right to focus first and foremost on your own vulnerability journey. By default, that will influence the dynamics that you engage in. More often than not, it will influence them for the better. When you interact with people who are as committed to their inner work as you are to yours, it will make for a phenomenal combination. But at times people may react negatively to your lead. For example, they might get offended by your boundaries because they don't have a healthy sense of boundaries themselves. They might recoil at your authenticity because of their own shame, which prevents them from dropping facades. And this is not your responsibility. These are their triggers and projections.

However, you *can* know where your responsibility starts and ends in your relationships (hello self-trust and discernment) and consciously choose to encourage the best possible outcomes. Learning how to hold space for others while simultaneously holding space for yourself will set you up for the greatest chance of success.

It takes mastery to do this. It requires striking the right balance between honoring your own needs and honoring the needs of the other person. To speak and listen with intention. To be in tune with both your experience and theirs—in real time, mid-conversation—and adjust your communication accordingly. Throw in emotionally charged moments and the unconscious mechanisms humans use to shield themselves from vulnerability, and you can understand why this process is a journey.

In the ultimate vulnerability vision you set for yourself in Chapter 1, it's possible that you saw yourself embodying this kind of skillful interpersonal grace. Improving your ability to be a safe space for others will help bridge the gap between where you are now—and you've already come far!—and your ultimate vision. This is why being able to receive vulnerability is as key as being vulnerable yourself.

REFLECTION

1. On a scale of 1 to 10, how would you rate your ability to hold space for others? (Here, 1 would mean feeling completely unable to accept the vulnerability of others, reacting by shutting down, shaming them, changing the topic, or even attacking them; 10 would mean being the kind of person that even strangers feel naturally inclined to open up to—others tending to trust you with their innermost thoughts and feelings, and you feeling quite comfortable in that role.)

1	2	3	4	5	6	7	8	9	10

2. On a scale of 1 to 10, how comfortable are you with displays of vulnerability? (Here, 1 would mean feeling extremely uncomfortable, to the point of wanting to extract yourself from the situation; 10 would mean feeling that you naturally know how to respond with just the right words and actions.)

1	2	3	4	5	6	7	8	9	10

THE VULNERABILITY WORKBOOK

3. Have you ever received feedback about the way you react when people confide in you or express vulnerable things to you? If so, what kind of feedback? Do you agree with what was said? Why or why not?

1	2	3	4	5	6	7	8	9	10

What Being a Safe Space for Others Entails

Organizational researchers and leadership experts have been interested in the idea of psychological safety in the workplace for the past few decades. According to Amy Edmondson, professor of leadership and management at Harvard Business School, team psychological safety is "a shared belief held by members of a team that the team is safe for interpersonal risk taking."[17]

This idea is super-relevant in relationships, too. In the definition above, replace the word "team" with "relationship" and you've got a breeding ground for vulnerability. In a psychologically safe relationship, people share the belief that the relationship is safe for interpersonal risk-taking. In other words, it's a safe space to be vulnerable even when it's scary.

Psychological safety in teams leads to better performance outcomes. When leaders nurture it, team members feel more comfortable sharing thoughts and ideas, trying new things, and learning and growing without fearing negative repercussions. This drives positive results, such as increased innovation and reduced turnover. And the same can be said about psychological safety in relationships. When you lead in ways that foster psychological safety, you'll enjoy better relationships.

To hold space for others, think of yourself as a leader aiming to create psychological safety. Read on for a few tips to try in your interactions.

Give Permission

"Permission to say or ask anything is priceless. It allows us to fully express ourselves: to seek what we want, to give feedback, to speak up about issues when we find the need," wrote author, speaker, and corporate trainer Paul Axtell in a *Harvard Business Review* article[18] about making meetings a safe space. This is another great piece of wisdom that extends beyond the world of management into interactions of any kind.

---

17 Amy Edmondson, "Psychological Safety and Learning Behavior in Work Teams," in *Administrative Science Quarterly* 44, no. 2 (1999): 350–83. https://doi.org/10.2307/2666999.
18 Paul Axtell, "Make Your Meetings a Safe Space for Honest Conversation," in *Harvard Business Review*, April 11, 2019. https://hbr.org/2019/04/make-your-meetings-a-safe-space-for-honest-conversation.

Giving others permission to share whatever comes up sends the message that their vulnerability is welcome, and that they should not fear your reaction to it. It opens the door for sharing. Whether others want to take you up on it is up to them, and it's important not to pressure them into sharing. Wondering what giving permission looks like? Here are a few statements inviting people into vulnerable conversations:

- "I am here for you if you want to talk about it."

- "Just so you know, you can be honest with me no matter what. Open communication is so important to me, and I want you to know that there's nothing we can't talk about."

- "If you are comfortable sharing more, I would love to hear about it."

- "I am noticing that you seem a little _____. Am I reading you correctly? Is everything okay? You don't need to share, but I am here if you want to."

- "Everything that we talk about stays between us, and I will listen without judgment."

Stay Curious

If you want to be a safe space for others, it's not just about what you say. Your intention and energy in the interaction speak more loudly than words. For that reason, it's crucial to approach conversations with curiosity rather than judgment.

We all judge. It's human nature to give meaning to things and to draw conclusions based on our own values and experiences. Accepting that fact will make you more aware of your own judgments so that you can stay curious throughout a conversation. Staying curious looks more like being a scientist conducting an experiment than being a lawyer arguing a case. Don't make assumptions. Don't jump to conclusions. Seek to understand what the other person is sharing with you while being aware of your own biases.

Practice Active Listening

Part of the process of staying curious throughout a vulnerable interaction is listening in order to understand instead of listening in order to respond. Think of the scientist-versus-lawyer analogy above. The scientist is seeking to observe and take notes. The lawyer is seeking to argue a case. We are all so used to thinking about what we are going to say next in a conversation while the other person is still talking. Some people also listen to solve problems and give advice. But that's not really listening. Ask for permission or wait until being solicited before you offer advice.

Listening to understand changes everything in the dynamic of a conversation. All of a sudden you hear things that you weren't paying attention to before. And the person talking to you feels truly heard and inspired to share more meaningfully, and then to pay back the favor.

To listen in that way is one of the skills required for "active listening," a concept you may already have heard about. Active listening works wonders for creating psychological safety and encouraging vulnerability. And it also involves the way you respond—what you say and how you say it. It is "a pattern of listening that keeps you engaged with your conversation partner in a positive way. It is the process of listening attentively while someone else speaks, paraphrasing and reflecting back what is said, and withholding judgment and advice," according to Arlin Cuncic in an article for Verywell Mind.[19]

ACTIVITY

For the next few days, practice active listening in all your conversations. Notice when you are listening to respond instead of listening to understand, and adjust accordingly. Paraphrase what people share with you and reflect it back to them. For instance, if someone shares with you that they are stressed out because they fought with their partner, you might say something like "I understand. You are feeling stressed today because the unresolved conflict is weighing on you."

Receive with Empathy and Validation

Active listening is powerful, because when you reflect back what a person is saying, you are actively demonstrating empathy and validation. This sends the signal that you are a safe space.

The Merriam-Webster dictionary defines empathy as "the action of understanding, being aware of, being sensitive to, and vicariously experiencing the feelings, thoughts, and experience of another of either the past or present without having the feelings, thoughts, and experience fully communicated in an objectively explicit manner."

When you can put yourself in the other person's shoes and they sense that in your body language and responses, they feel good after being vulnerable with you. The opposite is also true. If you are completely unable to empathize with their experience and that shows in your reactions, they will instinctively want to retreat and share less.

---

19 Arlin Cuncic, "What Is Active Listening?" Verywell Mind, updated February 13, 2022. https://www .verywellmind.com/what-is-active-listening-3024343.

As for validation, the idea here is that everything someone else feels is valid, whether or not you agree with it. Empathizing with and validating a statement doesn't mean that you agree with it, but that you respect and appreciate the other party's experience. When you receive information with both empathy and validation, others can feel that it's safe to be vulnerable with you—that you won't judge them or reject them for it.

Be Aware of Your Triggers and Projections

At times it can be challenging to stay empathetic and curious, and to offer validation. That's because of the triggers and projections you learned about in Chapter 7. Sometimes what people share will trigger you and bring up strong and uncomfortable emotions. At other times you will project your own inner conflict onto others. This is absolutely to be expected—you wouldn't be human otherwise. To be a safe space for others, however, do your best to be self-aware during interactions so that you can recognize when this is happening and self-regulate before you respond.

It's also absolutely acceptable (and vulnerable) to admit that you are triggered and to share this with someone. It's part of authentic communication. Context is important here, so use your discernment to evaluate whether it is appropriate and relevant to share that you're triggered. If so, you might say something such as "I'm sorry if I seem a little tense or angry. What you are sharing is triggering me because_____, but it has nothing to do with you. Thank you for being so open with me."

This also helps others feel psychologically safe with you. Being willing to be vulnerable yourself and to share things such as triggers shows that you aren't trying to maintain a facade of perfection, and that you are less likely to judge. It also means that you trust the other person, and it sends the cue that you are willing to engage in an authentic interaction in which mutual trust is valued.

REFLECTION

1. What are your biggest challenges when it comes to being a safe space and creating psychological safety for others? For example, you may have a tendency to give advice and try to find a solution to what the other person is telling you instead of actively listening. How can you work on areas needing improvement?

_____

_____

_____

_____

_____

2. What are your biggest strengths when it comes to being a safe space and creating psychological safety for others? Perhaps you are naturally empathetic and can tune in to the emotions of others and relate to them. How can you build on those strengths?

_____

_____

_____

_____

_____

In light of your responses to the previous questions, what can you do to improve your ability to be a safe space for others? Pick one or two skills and aim to incorporate them into your interactions as you move forward.

Holding Space for Others—in Action

The idea of "holding space" can sound abstract at times, but it's very much a skill. Explore how this skill can be put into action through the case studies below.

CASE STUDY 1

Zahra and Constance have been best friends since childhood. They are very different, personality-wise: Zahra is an artist, while Constance is a financial analyst. Zahra loves to go out, and Constance is a homebody. Zahra is also very in tune with her emotions and the emotions of others, while Constance prefers dealing with facts. In the past few months, Zahra has been getting a bit frustrated about the dynamic of their relationship. She's always accepted Constance for who she is, and she loves how supportive of each other they have been throughout the years. But their interactions have been challenging of late.

Zahra is going through a stressful time; she recently got fired from her job, and on top of that she has to move out of her apartment and find a new one. She has tried to confide in Constance and share just how much all these sudden changes have affected her. The first time, Constance seemed distracted. She kept looking at her phone and then abruptly cut their dinner short without realizing how much that hurt Zahra, who was in the middle of telling her about her apartment-hunting. The second time, Zahra became really vulnerable and shared that she had a deep-rooted fear of ending up homeless. Constance laughed and told her not to be dramatic. This made Zahra regret having opened up.

1. In what ways is Constance failing to hold space for Zahra?

2. How is this affecting Zahra?

3. How could it affect their relationship?

4. How could Constance create psychological safety in her interaction with Zahra?

....

....

....

....

5. What could Constance say to give Zahra permission to be vulnerable?

....

....

....

....

6. What could she say to make Zahra feel heard, empathized with, and validated?

....

....

....

....

Gary trains at the gym in his work building. He is a regular—every day at lunchtime he heads to the gym and works out. He often crosses paths with other colleagues there, including Kyle, the only one as assiduous about his fitness routine as he is. Gary and Kyle usually exchange brief hellos or chit-chat if they bump into each other in the locker room.

Today Gary notices something different. First, Kyle barely looked at Gary when he waved from afar. Then, in the weight room, Kyle cut his workout short and got up to leave. Gary knows Kyle is as disciplined about his workout routine as he is, so it was unusual behavior. He just has a feeling that Kyle isn't okay, so he decides to check on him. He catches up with him in the hallway. "Hey man, is everything all right? Noticed you seem a little off today." Kyle sighs and responds, "Honestly, not really. My girlfriend left me last night." Gary feels a pang of empathy. He remembers when he was in a similar situation. "I am so sorry," he responds, looking at Kyle warmly. "I completely understand how you feel—my ex left me two years ago, and I was devastated. I'm here if you want to talk about it."

1. In what ways did Gary hold space for Kyle?

2. How did Gary create psychological safety for Kyle?

3. What did Gary do to demonstrate active listening?

4. What did Gary do to demonstrate empathy?

5. How could this interaction positively affect their relationship?

Nora is having lunch with her younger brother, Anthony. They don't live in the same city, but he is in town for work, so they are using this opportunity to catch up. Anthony has always been the funny one in the family—he cracks jokes everywhere he goes. So when all of a sudden he gets serious mid-conversation, Nora senses he is about to share something important.

"I am going to ask Lily to marry me. I feel so excited but so nervous, too," Anthony says. Nora tries to smile and show excitement, but she feels a deep discomfort brewing within her. While Anthony shares more details about how he is planning to propose, she notices that she feels upset. She feels the urge to interrupt and share concerns. But the truth is, Nora has been with her own partner for seven years and he still hasn't proposed. She is resentful about it and can't believe that Anthony is proposing to Lily after two years—and they are way younger than she is. Nora realizes where her feeling of discomfort is coming from.

This is an important moment for her brother, and he is usually not that open with her about his personal life. She wouldn't want to discourage him from opening up in the future. She steers herself back to the present moment and listens intently. "I love your idea for the proposal—surprising her during your vacation will be super romantic. What kind of ring are you thinking of getting?"

1. In what ways did Nora use self-awareness, discernment, and self-regulation during her conversation with Anthony?

....

....

....

....

2. How did that help her hold space for him?

_____

_____

_____

_____

3. How did Nora demonstrate active listening once she steered herself back to the present moment?

_____

_____

_____

_____

4. How might the interaction have gone had Nora been less self-aware?

_____

_____

_____

_____

Chapter 10

REFLECTING ON WHAT YOU'VE LEARNED AND RECOMMITTING

In the final steps of the hero's journey, the reward is finally obtained: a treasure, knowledge, or whatever else was the catalyst for the original quest. Then begins the road back home. The hero has achieved what he or she set out to do, but the journey is not quite over at this point. It may include other tests and challenges right before the triumphant hero returns to the ordinary world, bearing the wisdom of transformation—and ready to share it with the world.

The same can be said about your own vulnerability journey. At this point you have seized some rewards. But it's not quite over. As you apply your tools and insights in real life, you may encounter challenges. Some interactions will be easier than others. You may feel fantastic about communicating authentically, setting boundaries. and being vulnerable in one conversation, then catch yourself resorting to unhelpful patterns that protect you from shame in the next one. You will learn more about yourself and others as you notice such things. In turn, you will feel more connected to yourself and others in the process. The important thing is to keep moving forward and gently observing whatever comes up, without beating yourself up or aiming for some sort of perfect vulnerability end game. At times, living with courage and vulnerability will feel like one step forward and two steps back. This is all to be expected.

So if there is no perfect vulnerability end game, what does the final stage of this hero's journey look like? If you remember the vision that you set for yourself in Chapter 1, that's what it looks like. But it's a bit of a paradox. To embody the version of yourself from that ultimate vulnerability vision, you have to view vulnerability as a moment-to-moment process instead of a finish line. Once you do so and you aim to stay aware and practice what you've learned, one moment at a time, you'll notice that the pillars from this workbook will start to just "click" as part of your natural way of being.

The paradox is also that if you start to judge yourself for not being "good enough" at vulnerability, you'll start to move away from it. In Chapter 9 you dived into the idea of holding space for others and creating psychological safety through such practices as listening with curiosity instead of judgment. It's the same when you hold space for yourself. Focus on understanding yourself instead of being critical, and that will foster the inner safety required to take the risk of being vulnerable.

Think of it this way. If you feel like the version of yourself from your ultimate vulnerability vision at least 50 percent of the time, you are doing a fantastic job. It's about aiming to live your vision every day, steering yourself back toward it when you're not doing so—continuously, throughout different seasons of life and in various situations. Then it will feel like an embodiment of vulnerability. That's the hero's transformation.

It's also likely that—just as heroes in epic stories do upon their return—you'll feel passionate about sharing your life-changing transformation with others. Don't be surprised if you inspire those around you to follow in your footsteps. This is the beautiful aspect of traveling this path: As you show up in the world embodying the principles that you have developed through this workbook, a ripple effect takes place. This ripple effect inspires and moves others to embrace vulnerability despite their own fears. And it creates a better world—one that is more connected, meaningful, free, loving, and authentically expressed.

REFLECTION

1. Read your Chapter 1 vulnerability vision and intentions again. How do you feel now about what you wrote?

....

....

....

....

....

THE VULNERABILITY WORKBOOK

2. In what ways do you already find yourself embodying that version of yourself and those intentions?

_____

_____

_____

_____

_____

3. In what areas do you think there are still gaps to bridge? Why?

_____

_____

_____

_____

_____

4. Do you find yourself being a perfectionist about your vulnerability journey? If so, how can you invite more compassion and curiosity along your journey? For example, you can decide that if you are vulnerable at least once a day, that is okay for now, as long as you keep showing up. Or you may focus on paying attention to your inner dialogue when you try to be vulnerable in order to notice what thought patterns come up.

5. What are some ways in which you can steer yourself back to your vision and intentions when needed? For example, you could journal daily for five minutes to connect with yourself on a deeper level. In your journal, you could look back on your interactions, how you felt, and how you acted with others that day to understand whether or not you have embodied your vision and intentions.

THE VULNERABILITY WORKBOOK

Create a personalized daily ritual that will help you stay aligned with your vision and intentions. This can be a simple habit or reminder to practice vulnerability without aiming for perfection or judging yourself. The five-minute journaling practice suggested above is a good example. You might also choose a symbol, such as a bracelet, as a visual cue to stay on your vulnerability journey and practice the guiding principles from this workbook.

Making the Most of This Workbook

The reflections and activities in each chapter of this workbook have been designed to give you tools and a new way of approaching things rather than definitive answers or conclusions. You could go through the process again in six months or a year and end up with very different answers and practices. And that's the beauty of this process.

Embracing vulnerability is contextual. It depends on who you are at a given point in your life, whom you are vulnerable with and when, and how you go about it. The way your fears of vulnerability show up also can vary depending on the context. In addition to all that, the external world is constantly changing and evolving, and so are you. That's why you've focused on setting intentions, acquiring tools, and embodying guiding principles instead of looking for a vulnerability operating manual.

If you feel inclined to revisit this vulnerability work, feel free to go through the entire workbook again or zoom in on specific chapters. Perhaps authentic communication just clicked for you, but you feel the most challenged when you have to manage intense emotions. That's when going back to a chapter or two could help. Maybe you feel way more comfortable being vulnerable after completing this workbook, until you encounter a new situation—like falling in love for the first time after divorce. That's when you might decide to go through the whole workbook again, this time answering the reflection questions and practicing the activities based on how you want to show up in that new relationship.

REFLECTION

1. Which chapters of this workbook have been the most impactful for you? Why?

....

....

....

....

....

....

....

2. Which chapters have been the most challenging for you? Why?

....

....

....

....

....

....

....

THE **VULNERABILITY** WORKBOOK

3. How has this process affected your relationship with yourself? Perhaps you are more aware of your thoughts and actions. Maybe you feel more comfortable dealing with shame when it comes up.

4. How has this process affected your relationships with others? Maybe dating has become more enjoyable. Perhaps you have deepened your bonds with your coworkers.

5. What has surprised you the most about this process?

6. What are the top three things you've learned and are taking with you as you move forward?

7. What are the top three habits that you are taking with you as you move forward?

_____

_____

_____

_____

_____

_____

_____

Celebrating and Integrating

Congratulations! The very act of completing this workbook is a display of tremendous courage and vulnerability. Celebrate yourself for being willing to get out of your comfort zone, unpack such constructs as your own shame and triggers, and put yourself out there even when it feels messy and icky. This is what vulnerability is all about, and getting to the end of this workbook is a testament to your transformation—even if you sometimes feel like a deer in the headlights when you attempt to be vulnerable. In fact, if you feel like that, it's a sign that you are doing something right!

Because of the nature of vulnerability and the emotional exposure that it entails, it might never feel super comfortable and easy to be vulnerable. If it did, this wouldn't be an act of vulnerability in the first place. But the tools that you carry with you will help ground you and create a sense of inner safety as you navigate outer uncertainty. And while vulnerability might always be uncomfortable to some degree, your window of tolerance for it will increase. Things that used to feel terrifying will barely faze you. And you'll find yourself feeling braver and taking bigger risks when warranted.

Few experiences are as freeing as doing something bold and vulnerable and realizing that you are okay on the other side of your fears. And not just okay—proud, unstoppable, alive, exhilarated, powerful, or any other state that encapsulates the burst of confidence, freedom, joy, love, and connection you feel when you dare to be your whole self and to express what that looks like in any given moment. Flaws and all, regardless of the outcome.

Remember that you get to access more and more of these moments as you keep showing up in the way you have through the pages of this workbook. Stay intentional in your interactions and connected to yourself. Revel in embracing vulnerability a little bit more every day. The real treasure is who you become in the process.

REFLECTION

1. Take a moment now to celebrate yourself and write down 10 vulnerability wins that you've experienced, big or small. A conversation where you were able to set a boundary could be a win for you, just as an improved marriage could be.

THE VULNERABILITY WORKBOOK

2. Use the next few pages to free-write about your learnings and reflect on the work you've completed in this workbook. Include any areas you want to keep exploring as you look ahead on your vulnerability journey.

THE **VULNERABILITY** WORKBOOK

THE VULNERABILITY WORKBOOK

ACKNOWLEDGMENTS

This book is based on my own vulnerability journey, which has been shaped with the help of therapists, mentors, and coaches throughout the years. I would particularly like to thank Dr. Rachel Toledano for changing the course of my life in my early twenties and planting the seeds of interest in psychology and human behavior. A special thank you to Dr. Alexis Shepperd for helping me unpack some of the more nuanced aspects of being vulnerable and supporting me in creating a deeper level of authentic self-expression and intimacy in my relationships. I would also like to express my deepest gratitude to my mom, Athina, who taught me how to read at the age of four and has always supported my dreams, including my writing endeavors. And a huge thank you to the team at Ulysses Press for their support.

ABOUT THE AUTHOR

Anouare Abdou is an author, authentic success mentor, and entrepreneur who started her career as a lifestyle journalist before stepping into leadership roles at websites like AskMen and Goalcast. From managing editorial teams to producing video content and leading business operations, she has tackled various challenges in digital media and discovered her passion for management in the process.

But despite her career success, it's her own relational trauma that led her on a powerful journey of self-discovery with one goal in mind: to be able to have happy, healthy relationships, because what's authentic success without them? Through years of therapy and healing modalities, she picked up tools and techniques that allowed her to transcend her limitations and create deeply fulfilling relationships. Now she's on a mission to help others do the same.

Anouare holds a BA in multiplatform journalism and is the coauthor of the best-selling book *Success Codes: Secrets to Success You Weren't Taught in School*. She lives in Montreal, Canada, and will happily skip the small talk to spend hours discussing philosophy and the nature of human behavior—preferably over a nice glass of wine and a good meal.